None of us is immune to stress and the mind's propensity to lose focus and attach itself to a myriad of arising thoughts and distractions. Thus, anyone can benefit from the teaching offered here. To quote Thompson, "We can interrupt the natural course of thoughts and emotions by bringing mindfulness to them. By doing so, we remove the kindling for the fire."

—Sharon Salzberg, author of *Lovingkindness and Real Love*

In this very helpful book, Logan Thompson illuminates the all too familiar patterns and causes of stress, particularly associated with test taking but equally applicable to the many other challenges of our lives. Drawing on many years of mindfulness training and teaching test prep, Logan offers extremely practical tools for understanding and relieving those habits of mind that limit our potential. *Beyond the Content* is written with graceful simplicity, warmth of heart, and transforming wisdom.

—Joseph Goldstein, author of *Mindfulness: A Practical Guide to Awakening*

This book helped me eliminate the unnecessary mental clutter brought on by the daunting nature of standardized tests.

—Sharon, student

Anxiety can inhibit performance even if you understand the test material. Logan's book teaches you to overcome this anxiety and perform at your very best.

—Jonathan Schneider, Director of Academics, Manhattan Prep

Beyond the Content is a wealth of resources. Logan provides practical and playful ways to help students succeed not only in test prep but in life skills such as how to relax while fervently pursuing a goal.

—Jessica Morey, Executive Director of Inward Bound Mindfulness Education (iBme)

BEYOND
the
CONTENT

Mindfulness as a
Test Prep Advantage

LOGAN THOMPSON

Illustrations by Cara Lai.

© 2019 Logan Thompson

Published by Kaplan Publishing, a division of Kaplan, Inc.
750 Third Avenue
New York, NY 10017

ISBN: 978-1-5062-4847-9

10 9 8 7 6 5 4 3 2 1

Acknowledgments

Joseph Goldstein and Tara Brach have served as endlessly patient meditation teachers and mentors, and continue to show me the true meanings of wisdom, curiosity, and kindness. Jessica Morey first enabled and encouraged me to teach mindfulness to young adults on meditation retreats. Jonathan Schneider first enabled and encouraged me to incorporate mindfulness into a test prep classroom. Chris Ryan served as a soundboard, advisor, and editor during this book-writing process. My students have bravely subjected themselves to multiple iterations of the system I've outlined in this book and have provided invaluable feedback. Yet, without the consistent faith and support from my mother, all of the above would have only amounted to a collection of unrealized opportunities.

TABLE OF CONTENTS

Preface

My sister Maisie recently came up here to Boston for a big jiu-jitsu competition. She weighs all of 105 pounds and can pretty much take me.

The day before her tournament, she asked me what she should do about her busy mind. She said that she had sparred in practice for months but couldn't remember being this nervous. She sounded like most of my test prep students, who tend to get more nervous for test day than for practice-test day.

Maisie said that her mind was like a rave, a disorienting onslaught of noise and emotion. I asked her if she could identify the loudest and most persistent themes of her mind. She said that the main two were: *What if your opponent does something you haven't thought of?* and *What if you forget all your training?*

Maisie had recognized a kind of *passenger* in her head. Each of us has many. I explained that underneath their single-minded rants and misguided tactics, passengers actually have our best interests at heart. I said, "Maisie, I *hope* you have a passenger that's trying to keep you alive. I'm glad it's speaking up. It's just not doing so in a balanced way. You can hear your passenger's concern without giving in to its panic."

By acknowledging and genuinely listening to our passengers, we can often lessen the anguish that they can cause. To some degree, the passengers will feel like they can put down their megaphones.

Maisie calmed as we continued talking, and as I told her more about the concepts of passengers and drivers, which are central to this book.

The next day, the day of the tournament, Maisie said that she was feeling much better about competing. Because I was writing this book at the time, I was curious about which parts of our conversation had helped her the most.

She said, "I don't know. I still hear all those 'what if' voices and the overanalyzing and the fear, but it's okay because it's just mind stuff."

It's just mind stuff.

I love that. Maisie had realized that there was no way to banish her passengers. So she accepted their presence, without necessarily accepting their particular prescriptions.

Once relieved of the fight with her passengers, she was able to concentrate on the fight with her opponent. She had mental and physical bandwidth to remember all of her training and to give herself support. I told her that this self-supportive part of her was her *driver*—the core part of each of us that contains tremendous wisdom and kindness.

Maisie ended up winning her matches by submission and taking home the gold. For the next month, she trained hard and continued to engage in many of the practices in this book. She went on to win the silver medal in the September 2018 world championship.

As Maisie was, you are now preparing for an important, stress-inducing event. Not unlike a jiu-jitsu tournament, a standardized test requires both a strong skill set *and* a strong mindset.

With this book, you can learn to identify and overcome your passengers as Maisie did. And you can learn to strengthen and call upon your driver, as Maisie did.

Before we begin, I'd like you the reader to know that I will be sharing several anecdotes about my students—students of various ages, studying for various standardized tests. Because the techniques in this book are *equally* applicable to a 15-year-old studying for the SAT and a 40-year-old studying for the MCAT, I will not be divulging the age of the students I write about, nor the test each one is preparing for. Hopefully, this will better allow you to see yourself in each of the cases presented.

CHAPTER 1

Content and Strategy Are Not Enough

Death, Taxes, and Test Prep

You know how people say there are two guarantees in life, death and taxes? One could make an argument for a third category: standardized tests. We're all in the same boat. We all have to fight this huge monster. But no one is telling you that you're doing it with one hand tied behind your back. I'm here to tell you how to use your other hand.

Every classroom I've been in focuses on two things: content and strategy. But those aren't the only things at play during a test. At times, I have mastered the content and the strategy and have still bombed a test. Dozens of my students have had the same experience, complaining, "I have memorized everything I'm supposed to know, and I get most of the problems right during my homework. But I just can't perform the same way on the test."

Have you ever missed a problem on a test that you "should" have gotten right, saying to yourself something like, "I *know*

I know this!"? Carla, a student of mine, had exactly this happen to her. She told me that she just couldn't figure out the problem. But we both knew that she knew the exponent rules. And yet she said that her mind was blank.

It would be understandable for a teacher to want to prescribe more exponents practice. After all, Carla was having trouble with exponents, right? However, a mind going blank is often unrelated to content knowledge. It can be a sign of being overwhelmed. When I inquired, Carla told me that in the back of her mind, she was terrified that she wouldn't perform well on the test and, therefore, wouldn't get into school. After acknowledging and working with that fear in several of the ways I will outline in this book, Carla's body and mind settled, giving her access to the content she already had stored.

Lacking an understanding or even an awareness of this under-the-surface phenomenon, students often turn on themselves. They think, *If I'm doing everything the textbook says and everything my teacher says, and I'm* still *failing, it must be me. I must be the failure.* It's natural for us to fill the gap between expectations and performance with self-criticism and self-blame. But those are temporary fillers that don't offer any dependable solution.

The Other Half of Test Prep

What is this other thing, besides content and strategy, that matters so much? What is this ever-present, rarely mentioned elephant in the classroom? *The other half of test prep.*

The other half of test prep is the world of fleeting thoughts and emotions, always flickering, always murmuring inside your head, usually going unnoticed and unremarked upon.

Individually, these thoughts and emotions last just an instant. They're like sparks from a campfire, flying up and dimming out a moment later. Collectively, though, these streaming sparks in our mind are very powerful. They shape our perceptions and perspectives. And they dictate our performance on tests.

We don't often talk about the other half of test prep, if ever. We don't talk about those nagging voices in our heads that tell us we can't do it. We don't talk about distracting thoughts taking our attention away. We don't talk about how fast a single kernel of self-doubt can sprout into a whole thicket of insecurities. We don't talk about how our bodies can hijack us and shut us down in shame or make us want to jump out of our skin with anxiety.

Whether you're a student or a teacher, it can be uncomfortable to talk about the other half of test prep. Some students think it's too personal or embarrassing. Some teachers don't feel qualified enough to broach the subject.

But ignoring the elephant doesn't make it go away. The other half of test prep is happening all the time, whether we like it or not. Your mental and emotional state, your surfacing memories, your underlying beliefs are always there. Like the aperture on a camera, your mind and body control the inflow and outflow of information. Depending on the state of the mind and body, that flow can be open, closed, or somewhere in between.

The good news is that by acknowledging the other half of test prep, exploring it, and working with it, you can gain access to your full potential. While this book focuses on test prep, there is no life arena that can't benefit from an enhanced awareness of this internal process.

Root Causes

Symptoms of the other half of test prep often masquerade or manifest as content related, because content is the only thing being directly measured. We even talk about the test only in terms of content. We say, "It's a geometry problem."

But it's not *just* a geometry problem. It's a geometry and a *you* problem. Everything about you is involved in solving that geometry problem. But we don't have easy metrics for the *you* part. We don't have students in an MRI machine in the classroom. We don't have students hooked up to biofeedback, EKGs, etc. So teachers rely on the most obvious metric available: *Did you get the problem right?* In our diagnosis of a student, we often only find content issues, because that's all we're looking for. We then prescribe you content homework based on the content issues we see, creating a feedback loop that often excludes the core learning issue. As Abraham Maslow wrote, "If all we have is a hammer, everything looks like a nail." Too often, as teachers, our tool belt only holds a content hammer.

When we don't address the root cause, the symptoms remain. It's as if you have a pain in your right hand that is actually caused by a pinched nerve in your neck. Massaging and icing your hand would give you only temporary relief, if that. How unfortunate would it be if you never found out that the pain was actually coming from your neck? Perhaps as unfortunate as never finding out that the reason for your poor performance in test prep was actually caused by something that neither you nor your teachers ever addressed.

A monk named Ajahn Sucitto once spoke of a tree's leaves as a metaphor for our daily issues in life. Negative issues—a sprained ankle, a botched interview, a breakup, a bad test score, etc.—would be represented by brown leaves. Sucitto said that an unwise person would try to use green paint on the brown leaves, thinking that doing so would restore the health of the tree. The wise person would water the roots of the tree, even though that doesn't immediately and directly address the brown leaves.

If you ever feel like you're spinning your wheels in a certain test area, ask yourself if you are just painting the leaves. For example, if you get a bunch of geometry problems wrong even though you know all of the formulas and strategies, doing a bunch more geometry problems would probably be painting the leaves.

You will need to be extra vigilant about this. Sometimes well-intentioned teachers will assign homework that is equivalent to painting the leaves, simply because they aren't trained in the other half of test prep.

By no means am I saying that learning the content is not important. It's essential. It's just not enough. An old boss of mine used to say, "It's like speed in sports. It is necessary but not sufficient."

You still need the first half of test prep: content and strategy. After all, it is half of test prep. There are tens of thousands of great resources out there about the first half of test prep, so I'm going to focus the next hundred or so pages on the other half.

Enhancing the Positive, Reducing the Negative

Some people work with a physical therapist to fix their bodies in some way. Other people don't need to "fix" anything but want to enhance their physical performance. Those people work with a physical trainer. Just because certain people don't need physical therapy doesn't mean that their bodies are at peak performing condition. Maybe they could still benefit from physical training.

Similarly, you might not suffer from test anxiety or critical thoughts. But does that mean your mind is serving you in the best way possible? Is it optimally focused? Calm? Energized?

Addressing the other half of test prep can both reduce the negative aspects and enhance the positive aspects of your mental performance, serving as your physical therapist *and* as your physical trainer.

Unhelpful thoughts and emotions accompany all of us, to some degree. Check for yourself. Has your mind been 100 percent clear and focused while reading the past few pages?

You may have retained most of what you read, but that doesn't mean that 20, 30, or 40 percent of your attention wasn't entertaining other thoughts and voices: *How is this stuff gonna help me do better on my test? Is he gonna talk about how to do a problem soon? Should I go to the gym? What's for dinner?*

Plinko

There's a game on the show *The Price Is Right* called Plinko. A contestant drops a Plinko chip, which looks like an oversized checker, down an inclined board that has horizontal pegs sticking out. Gravity forces the chip to fall onto several of those pegs, but only chance can tell which way that Plinko chip will go when it hits each peg. After hitting a dozen or so of these pegs, the Plinko chip ends up in one of several slots on the bottom. Each of the slots represents some sort of prize on the show.

Our mind-body process is not too unlike concurrent games of Plinko, each peg representing moments in our lives that disrupt our thoughts and lead us down different paths. Seeing a tree can quickly lead to regrets from a past relationship. Hearing construction can cause us to call for restaurant reservations. Stepping on a pebble can lead us to invest in a timeshare on the beach.

Consider the following scenario.

You're walking your dog down the street, and you both see a tree. The tree reminds you that you want to buy an indoor tree for your apartment. You start thinking of the different kinds of trees that would work in that corner of your bedroom. Your mind sees the picture hanging in that corner, which was a gift from your ex. You feel all of the emotions, including regret that you weren't more generous with your ex.

Meanwhile, you've only taken five steps since you first saw the tree, yet you have created and are now fully living in an entirely different universe, *without knowing it.*

How does this relate to the test? Every sensory input is like a Plinko chip—every thought, every problem you see, every itch you feel. Each one can lead us to states of mind we did not plan on visiting. Using the techniques in this book, we can learn to tilt that Plinko table more parallel to the ground, slowing down the chip's chaotic descent. We can guide that chip to more desired slots.

Now, imagine a Plinko board that somehow developed grooves of the most common chip paths, thereby making those paths more likely for new chips to take. That happens in our minds. If a cause-and-effect neural pathway is worn well enough, a stimulus will often lead us to the same place. Using mindfulness, over time, we can intimately learn each step in the mental flow chart, better allowing us to interrupt it at any given time, even at the very first cause-and-effect link.

The more we pay attention, the more we see that each stimulus and response, or cause and effect, often comprises multiple smaller cause-and-effect links. For example, if someone isn't paying very much attention, that person may think that seeing a tree led to relationship regrets. But it didn't. Seeing the tree led to something, which led to something else, which led to something else, which led to something else, which led to relationship regrets.

Bridget

Bridget is currently my tutoring student. She is an intelligent young woman, and she knows she's intelligent. But every time she would practice math, she would freeze in fear. Her mind would go blank, her heart would race, then she would sink in shame. She got so frustrated that she started avoiding math altogether. The experience of doing math was so horrific that her dread of that experience superseded her deep desire to increase her score.

I wanted to see Bridget's reaction in real time, so I visibly started a timer as I gave her a problem to do. I watched as Bridget's body tensed, as her eyes welled up with tears, as her hands started to tremble. Although my goal was not to cause her discomfort, I said, "This is awesome, Bridget!"

She was quite confused by my enthusiasm. But I told her that we had a wonderful opportunity to see what exactly was derailing her, in real time.

Here's a bit of our conversation:

Me: When did you notice a change from being calm to being stressed?

Bridget: I got scared as soon as the timer started. Then it just got worse and worse.

Me: What made you scared?

Bridget: That I would run out of time.

Me: Well, I'm gonna push back on that, because I could tell you that I'm going to time how long it takes you to go get a cup of water, and you wouldn't care. So it's not just being timed in and of itself that bothers you.

Bridget: Well, yeah. It's that if I can't do these problems in time, it means that I won't pass the test. So I just freak out when I do the problem.

Me: Which part of the problem? For example, do you freak out when you see words and numbers on a page? Or just when you think you don't have the answer? Or when you put your pen to paper?

Bridget: It's not during the reading part of the problem, or when I write . . . it's when I have to do it in my head.

Me: Why?

Bridget: I'm bad at mental math. People have always teased me about it. People at work still make fun of me for it.

Me: Ah, I see. And you think you should be good at it.

Bridget: Yeah.

Me: And you believe that if you aren't good at it, then you won't do well on the test.

Bridget: Yeah.

Me: And your coworkers will be proven right.

Bridget: Yeah.

Me: And you'll never get a promotion.

Bridget (now laughing through her tears): Yeah.

Me: So basically, because you can't do seventeen times eight quickly in your head, you're never going to amount to anything?

Bridget: Right!

Me: Never going to get into school?

Bridget: Right!

Me: Never going to be promoted?

Bridget: Exactly!

Me: Gonna be miserable forever?

Bridget (now laughing and emphatic): *Yes!* You think I'm kidding, but yes. That's exactly right! And I believe it even though it's ridiculous!

CHAPTER 2

Passengers and the Driver

What Is a Passenger?

I created the concept of *passengers* to help us get clarity on the amorphous and abstract thoughts and emotions in our minds. Without using the passenger system, I find that all the slippery little thoughts and emotions can be too ethereal to get a handle on. The idea of passengers helps us externalize thoughts and emotions, allowing them to be more understandable and workable. Through mindfulness, we can begin to recognize reoccurring themes of thoughts and emotions. Some are helpful. Some are not. We can call the ones that are not "passengers."

You may have heard someone say, "That's a part of myself I'm not proud of" or "That's my shadow side." These all refer to passengers. Our passengers are with us all the time. They may vary in number, in volume, in frequency of appearances, but we're never really alone. The presence of passengers is not a problem. The problems occur when we either don't recognize them or unquestioningly believe their messages. Passengers can be quite single-minded and persistent, and each one has a fervent message to share. The message itself may or may not be valuable, but the way in which passengers share that message is rarely helpful.

For example, if one of these passengers were in a real, physical car with you, that passenger would sound like, *Hey, you might want to turn left up here . . . turn left . . . hey . . . your whole whole purpose in life is to turn left . . . if you don't turn left, it's not even worth having a car or driving anywhere . . . hey, turn it to my favorite radio station; it's called turn left.*

We often hear these voices and messages subliminally, without realizing their effect on us. Unrecognized, these passengers can cause us to believe things and to behave in ways that are counter to our ultimate goals. It's critical not to view passengers as inherently bad. Just because they present as initially unhelpful doesn't mean that they are. They are actually coming from a caring place, and we can learn a lot from them.

Why Address Passengers?

Not seeing our passengers is like not seeing a literal car passenger is grabbing the wheel—not a good situation. When we don't see passengers, they control our lives. Everything we do is dictated by our thoughts and emotions, most of which arise without our permission or knowledge. Do you trust the wisdom of every thought that pops into your mind? While thoughts and emotions are fleeting, they often catalyze other thoughts and emotions. So one unrecognized thought can lead to a dramatic change in your state of mind thirty minutes later, and you may have no idea how you got there.

If you're driving, taking the wrong fork in the road is no big deal because you can just turn around and get back on track. But what if you don't realize that you took the wrong fork in the road? Then you can end up hundreds of miles away from your destination a few hours later.

In economics, there's a similar concept called the multiplier effect. The idea is that if you give someone a hundred dollars in some city, say, Birmingham, the economy of Birmingham usually expands by substantially more than a hundred dollars.

What happens is that the first person spends most, or all, of that hundred dollars in Birmingham. Then the people who received that money turn around and spend it. Where? Mostly in Birmingham. And this process continues. When you add up all the dominoes that fall in Birmingham, you get a lot more than a hundred dollars worth of economic activity. In essence, you've multiplied that initial hundred dollars by a number greater than one, known as a multiplier.

Unseen thoughts and emotions have a large multiplier effect, too. They unleash cascades of additional thoughts and emotions, causing potentially dramatic impact on our lives. So it's important to recognize our passengers, but it takes training. They're difficult for each of us to identify in our own minds. After all, the very lens through which we see them may be the lens of a passenger!

For example, if we operate from a place of believed inadequacy, objects independent of us can seem to have different qualities than they do when we operate from a place of believed self-worth. Following an elating experience, have you ever noticed the air suddenly feeling cleaner, food tasting better, colors seeming brighter? Nothing had actually changed about the air or the food or the colors. You simply had a different perception because of your state of mind/body.

What to Do About Passengers?

So what do we do about this situation? We're all in it. Passengers are part of our lives.

We have two choices. We can try to stop them from arriving. Or we can learn to deal with them, and even to make use of them.

Chances are that you've tried to stop a passenger. But that's about as successful as trying not to think about a pink elephant.

When passengers arise, we need to take four essential steps: **notice** them, **name** them, **engage** with them, and **welcome** them.

Notice

Before you identify an individual passenger, you need to learn to detect that a passenger is even present. The mere presence of passengers is no problem. It's our unwitting belief in their messages that causes so many problems.

Fortunately, there are a couple of telltale signs that passengers are running the show: (1) exiting our window of tolerance and (2) engaging in avoidance behaviors.

Exiting the Window of Tolerance

UCLA professor of psychology and executive director of the Mindsight Institute, Dr. Dan Siegel, describes our *window of tolerance* as a state of our minds and bodies when our activation level is just right. Not too wound up, and not too wound down.

We exit that window all the time. We call it *being really stressed*. If we look a little more closely, we exit that window in one of two directions.

1. *Up* is overstimulation, or hyperarousal. This is also known as fight or flight. Adrenaline courses through your body and brain. Your thoughts race. You feel anxious, jittery, hypervigilant.
2. *Down* is understimulation, or hypoarousal. This is also known as the freeze reaction. You have a pervasive sinking feeling, accompanied by dread, lethargy, and apathy.

The throes of test prep can cause either overstimulation or understimulation. To survive in the wild, our ancestors needed both of these reactions. Fight or flight allowed them to be ready to fight or flee at a moment's notice—if a wild animal or neighboring tribe attacked, for example. The freeze is just as useful. It kept them from being spotted by wild animals or enemies. It's sometimes called the *dorsal dive*, named after the dorsal vagus nerve that runs down our backs that activates the instinct to freeze. The dorsal dive is what allows marine mammals to dive and hold their breaths for so long.

Most of us live in a safe environment. Yet certain aspects of our daily lives, such as test prep, can cause our bodies to act as if we are being attacked by a lion. We can be in a classroom, clothed, fed, warm, surrounded by friends, and our bodies can act as if we're about to die. And I'm going to keep reminding you that it's not your fault. It's just remnants of evolution, misplaced. And it's manageable with the right training.

When we go into fight, flight, or freeze, needless to say, we become less effective at test prep. Our minds aren't expansive and creative. Fight or flight actually causes our vision to narrow, causes "the walls to close in." That said, *noticing* that you are exiting your window of tolerance is great news, because it means that you're probably believing a passenger. And I'm going to show you how to work with that. But first, you need to learn how to tell what part of the window of tolerance you are in at any given time.

EXERCISE

Are You in Your Window of Tolerance Right Now?

Set aside four minutes. Commit to not looking at your phone or surfing the Internet.

Guide your attention to three areas of your body, in the order below, assessing whether you are down and out of your window of tolerance, within your window of tolerance, or up and out of your window of tolerance.

Spend about 30 seconds just taking inventory of how these areas feel. You don't need to try to change how they feel. Just notice what's going on.

1. Belly/chest: Are they tense? Relaxed? Calm? Is your breathing shallow? Deep?

2. Throat/shoulders: Similarly, are they tight? Are your shoulders up near your ears or down and relaxed? Do your throat and/or shoulders feel open? Closed?

3. Face/jaw: Is your forehead furrowed? Is your jaw locked or open? Is your tongue pasted to the roof of your mouth or relaxed? Are the muscles around your eyes tense?

Overall, do you feel like you're energetically leaning forward, or are you relaxed and sitting back?

Now bring some awareness to your mind itself.

Does it feel open and clear or foggy and dull? Do you have racing thoughts? How positive or negative is the content of your thoughts?

Periodically taking inventory of your mental and physical state allows you to better assess where you are in relation to your window of tolerance.

It can be perfectly normal and even beneficial to experience some discomfort or anxiety during this process. It can lead to important insights about that very anxiety. Remember Bridget? I put a math problem in front of her and started the clock right after she told me she hated being timed. Was it wrong to time her? Not in and of itself. It all depended on whether she was in her window of tolerance.

You should start to learn your own signs of hyperarousal and hypoarousal. Discomfort, on its own, doesn't necessarily mean there's something wrong with what you're doing. Pushing yourself as you explore your own mind's processes is not necessarily wrong. In fact, it's often necessary for growth.

At the same time, it can be easy to adopt a kind of no-pain-no-gain attitude: *Just tough it out. No matter how bad it gets, just dig deeper and stay with it. Don't resist.* And so on.

The key is to listen to yourself. It's like figuring out the amount of pressure that's right for a massage. Sometimes you need a deep tissue massage, even if the targeted muscles end up aching. Sometimes you need a lighter Swedish massage. And sometimes your muscles may be too sore to be touched at all. If that's the case, they just need rest.

Stretching your window and playing with the edges are great things to try. Meditation teacher and author Tara Brach says, "Approach your edge, then soften." Blowing past your edge by digging too hard, too fast, and too deep isn't helpful. It just sends your body deeper into fight, flight, or freeze.

Think of a sports coach trying to help a player become more flexible. The coach will harm the player if the coach just leaps on the player's back. And the player won't become more flexible if the coach just lays a few fingertips on the player's back. The coach has to find the right middle ground—getting to the edge, then softening.

You have to be your own coach.

Engaging in Avoidance Behaviors

Engaging in avoidance behaviors is another common sign that you're listening to passengers. We all have these behaviors. To be honest, just now, while writing this section, I caught myself pouring a third bowl of cereal, and I'm not even hungry!

Eating, along with YouTube, are two of my go-to avoidance behaviors. When I catch myself doing either of them—especially if I haven't planned on doing them—I know to look for passengers I'm believing. In this case, I was believing a passenger who was telling me that I wouldn't meet the publication deadline for this book. Because I initially didn't notice that passenger, I implicitly believed its message, which was so uncomfortable that my body automatically decided to avoid the situation. Cereal just happened to be the outlet.

 **EXERCISE**

What Are Your Avoidance Behaviors?

Bring to mind something that you know you should do but really don't want to do. Maybe it's cleaning, studying, calling a relative, or having a difficult conversation with someone.

What are some things that you have done instead? Before reading on, take a few minutes to list some of your avoidance behaviors. Remember, these behaviors are going to be invaluable signals for you in the future.

Name

Have you ever had a lucid dream? This is when you wake up inside the dream. You're dreaming, but somehow you know you're in a dream. It's fascinating. Some people do it naturally, and some people apparently train themselves to do it. I've had several lucid dreams over the years. It's always bizarre to realize that the "people" I speak with in my dreams aren't actually other people. They're *me,* or part of my subconscious.

Once, when I was about sixteen years old, I had a dream in which I was running away from a tornado, terrified. Then I became lucid within the dream. I still felt the terror. At the same time, though, I knew the situation wasn't real. So I stopped running. I turned back to the tornado and asked it who it was. To my surprise, the tornado replied. It was someone I knew in real life. And then, as soon as the tornado was named, it shrank down and stopped chasing me. Dr. Dan Siegel refers to this amazing process as "name it to tame it." It works, and we need to do it with our passengers.

Naming our passengers acts as a recognition tool. It lets us categorize and grasp amorphous constellations of thoughts and emotions. Naming them allows us to more readily identify them, and even call on them later if needed. Naming our passengers also helps them understand that we really see them.

I recently read about a four-year-old and her dad. The four-year-old kept saying, "Daddy, Daddy, Daddy!" from her room. The dad let this go on for a little while and finally relented. When he went to her door and asked her what she needed, she giggled and told him to go away. She just needed to be seen.

Passengers can behave like four-year-olds. When they finally get our attention, even if it's momentarily, they often feel satisfied enough to retreat.

Simply bringing awareness to something or someone can be extremely powerful. You may have noticed this phenomenon when you were doing the exercise above to take inventory of your body and mind. Directing your attention to your shoulders, for instance, and asking whether they're tight, can cause them to release on their own.

When you suspect that there's a passenger present, ask yourself, *What thought or emotion is most uncomfortable?*

Which one are you most disturbed or shaken by? Which one might you be running from the most?

In *Romeo and Juliet*, Juliet famously asked, "What's in a name?" Well in this case, a lot. The name itself does matter, or rather the characteristics of that name. The name of each passenger should somehow reference the role of that passenger. So you probably shouldn't name your passenger *Patrick*. If it's a passenger that always tells you that you're too slow at everything, for example, you could name it *Big Ben* (after the tower clock in London).

The name should also be positive and lighthearted. Remember, these passengers are part of us. We only sabotage ourselves if we create an adversarial relationship with them. If we name a passenger *Really Annoying Voice*, for example, we significantly diminish our chances of successfully working with that passenger.

The point of naming passengers is to be able to recognize and step back from internal patterns, so there's no need to find a "perfect" name. That little bit of separation and recognition gives us space and room to breathe, allowing us to effectively work with our experiences. Let's practice naming one of your passengers. First, we'll need to call one up.

EXERCISE

Calling on Passengers

Gather a few challenging test prep problems in front of you. It doesn't matter what content area. Set a timer for yourself. Put a little bit of mental pressure on yourself. Tell yourself you have to get these problems right before the time runs out.

At the top of one page, write *Content*. At the top of the other page, write *Passengers*.

Next, start the clock and do the problem set.

Do your scratch work on the Content page.

Your ultimate goal is to keep your mental eyes and ears open to thoughts and emotions that aren't related to content or strategy. Half of your awareness should be on solving the problems. The other half of your awareness should be on noticing your internal dialogue and any accompanying emotions.

If you notice any potent or recurring mental activity during the problem set, pause for a moment. Write down what the voice is saying on the Passengers page. Briefly describe any accompanying physical sensations there as well.

After the timer goes off, take a minute to reflect and write about your experience. Again, use the Passengers page. Document any messages you may have heard.

I actually did this exercise with you. Here are my notes:

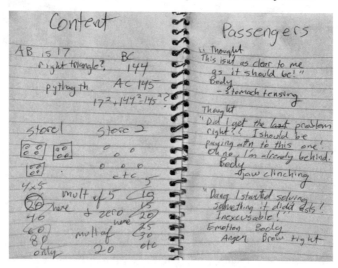

You may have noticed passengers; you may not have. If not, that's absolutely fine. Your internal "passenger detector" will strengthen as you continue through the exercises in this book.

Doing the above exercise every so often will help you identify and recognize prominent passengers. In fact, *any* stressful situation is likely to surface some of your passengers. If you have a "passengers page" ready in a small notebook that you keep with you, you can jot down what you notice there in real time, too.

Here are the thoughts I identified during the exercise:

- *This isn't as clear to me as it should be.* (Stomach tensed after this thought.)
- *Did I get the last problem right?*
- *I should be paying attention to this one!*
- *Oh no, I'm already behind.* (Jaw clenched after this thought.)
- *Dang, I started solving something it didn't ask! Inexcusable!* (Brow tightened after this thought.)

From these thoughts, I can name a few passengers.

Einstein: This passenger says I must always understand everything clearly right away, and if I don't, then the world will end.

Rearview Mirror: This passenger looks into my past to analyze—and overanalyze—my performance.

Big Ben: We named this passenger above, the one that points out over and over how slow I am.

But there's no need to name that many passengers in one exercise. In fact, I've only named about ten of mine, ever. You'll likely find that 20 percent of your passengers make 80 percent of the noise. So you only need to name five or ten. By design, the concept of passengers is simplistic and reductionistic. It's meant to help us familiarize ourselves with what's really going on in our minds. So the degree of specificity is an art, not a science.

I recommend staying with a smaller number of broader passengers. As you start to pay more attention, you will notice which passengers are most prevalent in your life. Keep in mind that you can always name new ones.

I'd like to name one more passenger, who derailed me the most during the exercise above. The "should" thought occurs fairly often to me and tends to lead to negative outcomes. Keeping in mind the two characteristics of a passenger name—descriptive and lighthearted—I think I'll name it *ShWoody*. I like the character Woody in the *Toy Story* movies, and I can picture little cartoon Woody telling me I should be doing something. That scenario is easy to imagine and causes little stress.

I recommend drawing, or at least imagining, your own cartoon version of a passenger (whether it is or isn't a cartoon already). Here's what Big Ben might look like.

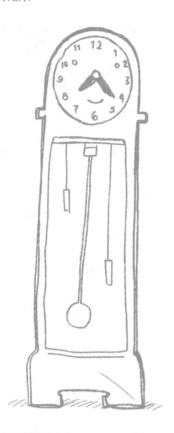

EXERCISE

Name and Draw a Passenger

Ask yourself which unhelpful thought patterns in the above exercise were most potent and/or frequent.

Name and sketch your first passenger!

Please feel free to steal any of mine. Most of us share several passengers. Just as there are popular archetypes in psychology and throughout history, most of our passengers are shared. So we may as well share their names also.

Sometimes identifying a passenger is enough to make it subside. As we will discuss more in the coming chapter on mindfulness, when thoughts are recognized and left to their own devices, they often dissipate on their own. It's the unseen, or implicitly believed, thoughts that tend to linger. So most of the time, internally saying, *Oh, hi, Big Ben!* is all you will need to do—no big project.

Engage

Sometimes passengers can make a bigger splash. Sometimes seeing and naming them is not enough to cause them to subside.

That's when we really need to understand, or re-understand, them. One of the benefits of naming passengers is that it creates the illusion of separation from them, enough of a separation for us to engage with them.

Just as we make assumptions about other people, it's easy to make assumptions about our passengers. About what they want, about their motivations and intentions. But when we probe a little deeper, we inevitably find a loving intention buried underneath the unhelpful words. This bears repeating. *All of our passengers, without fail, have a loving intention. If you can't find the loving intention, look harder.*

Shaking Branches

When I was fourteen years old, I had a big crush on a girl named Jessica. One day, my dad took me to a barbecue at her house, where I found myself talking to her under a tree. I really, really liked her. So, naturally, I grabbed a tree branch, wet from a recent rain, and shook it. In my mind, soaking her with rainwater would cause her to fall in love with me. It didn't.

The amazing thing is that I had no idea of my misstep until my uncle, who had witnessed the whole thing, gently said, "Ya know, Logo, it might not be the best idea to drench a girl with cold water when you're trying to flirt with her." Somehow that was news to me.

The point is that I had good intentions, but the impact was not so good. In fact, my good intentions were probably invisible to Jessica. Similarly, our passengers' good intentions are often invisible, at first glance, to us. So when we hear all that self-criticism, it's just our passengers shaking wet branches over our heads, because they really like us.

Talking To vs. Talking As

Understanding a passenger's motivation requires asking it questions. You have one goal when engaging a passenger: find out is its deepest loving motivation.

There are two ways to engage with a passenger. The first is to talk *to* it. The second is to talk *as* it. In other words, you put yourself in the passenger's shoes and speak your mind.

These two methods accomplish the same thing. So I recommend trying both and then using whichever one you feel more comfortable with. Talking *to* your passenger is probably more intuitive, because it's like talking to a person. The downside is that you kind of have to imagine its replies.

What do you actually say to the passenger? Just ask it what it wants for you. Very often this will be something that sounds pretty negative: *I want you to stop being terrible.* Or *I want you to be like other people.* Or *I don't want anything in particular; I just wanted to tell you that what you did is not good enough.*

Then you need to ask *why*. Ask until you find the good intention of the passenger.

Me: Why do you want me to stop being terrible?

Passenger: Because you're embarrassing yourself.

Me: Why don't you want me to embarrass myself?

Passenger: Because I want these people to like you.

Me: Why?

Passenger: Because I want you to belong to this group.

Me: Why?

Passenger: Because I don't want you to be cast out, which is painful and dangerous.

It will probably take more than a couple of questions, and perhaps more than a couple of attempts.

When talking *as* a passenger, you take both sides of the dialogue. Rather than imagining what the passenger would say, you take on the passenger's role yourself.

Here's me with my *should*-obsessed passenger ShWoody.

Me: Why do you keep telling me that I should be doing something different than I am doing?

(Now I'm imagining myself as this passenger.)

ShWoody: Because you're not doing something right, and you should do it right.

Me: Right, but why do you care?

ShWoody: Because it's just wrong when you do something wrong. You should have understood that problem sooner.

Me: Again, why do you care?

ShWoody: Because I don't want you to be getting a bunch of stuff wrong.

Me: Why?

ShWoody: Because you lost out on getting into the college you wanted to, and you lost out on a job you wanted, because you got things wrong in the interviews. And that sucked for you.

Me: Oh, so when you tell me I should be doing something different, it's just because you don't want me to feel pain that I've felt before?

ShWoody: Well, yeah.

Me: Oh. That's nice, I guess.

Because of conversations like these, my reactions to passengers have drastically changed. Sure, sometimes the messages do make me feel bad. But they rarely debilitate me anymore.

Sometimes understanding is enough to cause a passenger to subside. Have you ever been annoyed with the way someone else behaved around you? Maybe they teased you too much, or maybe they made a few jokes about you.

What happens in your mind when you get to know them better and find out that they're actually doing this teasing out of love, and that they only tease the people they care about the most? You may still not appreciate their behavior, but I'm guessing that your insight into their motivations probably takes some of the sting away.

That is what we want to accomplish with our passengers. Much of the time we have our guard up against our passengers. Which means we are guarded against ourselves. And when we are guarded, we lose access to our full potential. We are less creative, concentrated, empathetic, open to new ideas, and the list goes on and on. That's not good for most aspects of our lives. It's definitely not good for standardized test performance. On test day, we need all of our concentration, all of our creativity and openness, and all of our empathy and good will (particularly toward ourselves).

During your test prep process, I'm sure that passengers will continue to surface. Learn to notice them, name them, and engage with them, asking lots of "why" questions to surface their hidden good intentions for you. Passengers are bound to show up during your test. But they'll be pretty much the same ones you met during your prep. You'll want to know them already by name and really understand them.

That way, as the clock ticks down in the exam room, you'll be able to say, "Oh, hi!" to any passenger showing up, and then turn your attention relatively quickly back to solving the problem in front of you.

Stella

I just had a tutoring session with a student named Stella. Before she was referred to me, Stella had taken a test prep course and had engaged in several hours of private tutoring with another tutor. She repeatedly scored in the eightieth percentile on her practice tests, but couldn't seem to crack the sixtieth percentile on the official test. Stella had mastered the first half of test prep but hadn't tackled the other half yet. Here is part of our conversation.

Stella: I'm not an anxious person, but this test is making me crazy. I don't know what to do. My deadline is in two months.

(I spent some time introducing Stella to the concept of passengers and drivers, prompting her to ask the following.)

Stella: How am I supposed to know if the voice I'm hearing is a passenger or not? I mean, I just don't have as much potential to do well as others. That's not a passenger. That's just a fact.

Me: Passengers can be very convincing. During one mindfulness retreat, I asked one of my teachers, Brian Lesage, about a self-critical belief. Brian said, "Does that story make you feel bad about who you are?" I said, "Yeah." He said, "Then it's not all true." I laughed at the absurdity of his logic, "What do my subjective feelings have to do with the truth of an assertion?" But he wasn't laughing.

He went on to explain that while feelings don't *affect* the truth of an assertion, they do tend to *indicate* the truth of an assertion. He said, "Rather than take my word for it, I invite you to explore this yourself." I did, and he was right. I began to discover that when a thought or belief caused me to feel badly about who I was, it was generally a passenger.

So, Stella, a good place to start, when trying to determine whether the voice you are hearing is a passenger or driver, is to ask yourself, *Does the message make me feel bad about who I am? Does believing the message make my body feel sinking and contracted?*

If so, there is likely a passenger present.

Stella: You mentioned that this happened on a mindfulness retreat? What does mindfulness have to do with identifying passengers?

Me: The key word there is "identifying." Identifying requires noticing. Noticing requires awareness, which takes training.

When we practice mindfulness, we practice noticing thoughts and emotions that arise in any given moment. The more we train, the more things we notice, and the more often we notice them. And when we notice and identify passengers, they lose their power, because we can choose whether or not to believe what they say.

Stella: How will that help me on the test though?

Me: You said you were really stressed during the second section of the test because of how poorly you did on the first section.

Stella: It's gonna be really hard and stressful to identify and categorize all of those passengers.

Me: Yes, absolutely it can be, if you force it. Rather than saying to yourself, *Uh-oh, I'm a little stressed! I need to find and identify a passenger!,* say to yourself, *I'm a little stressed. Do I notice a theme to these thoughts and emotions? Can I easily and obviously identify a passenger? If not, no worries.*

Stella: Okay, so I just practice mindfulness and identify passengers?

Me: One last thing. You need to find the good intentions of the passengers that you identify.

Stella: What!? What is good about a passenger telling me I suck!?

Me: Well, nothing. I agree. But that doesn't mean the passenger wasn't *trying* to help. Imagine a dad watching his teenage daughter play basketball. The kid dribbles it off of her foot. So the dad yells at her harshly, telling her she has to work much harder at basketball. And when the daughter is older, she says, "Hey, Dad, why were you so hard on me?" The dad says, "I just wanted to make you stronger."

Good intentions don't necessarily mean that manifestations of those intentions are helpful. So it's up to us to find the helpful messages under the unhelpful ones. Finding and understanding those good intentions is the key to dealing with passengers effectively.

Welcome

Because passengers usually present as negative expressions of wholesome intentions, it may be tempting to just try to get rid of them. But that would just embolden them. The more we accept and embrace our passengers (which, remember, are parts of ourselves), the less intrusive the passengers become. We must adopt a welcoming attitude to all of our passengers, as Rumi describes in his poem *Guest House*. Here's an excerpt:

This being human is a guest house.

Every morning a new arrival.

A joy, a depression, a meanness,

some momentary awareness comes

as an unexpected visitor.

Welcome and entertain them all!

If you've done the previous exercises, you've named and drawn a passenger. You've engaged in conversation with it. Hopefully you've come to understand its good intentions.

When you encounter this passenger again, during a test prep session or at any other time, acknowledge it. Name it. And, remembering its good intention for you, welcome it. You don't have to heed its words, but embrace its intentions.

A Moment of Celebration

I want to highlight the scope of the undertaking you are embarking on. Our passengers have had direct access to our nervous systems for as long as we've been human. We are now questioning the validity of some of their messages. Remember that those "fight, flight, or freeze" messages have kept us alive as a species. If we failed to obey passengers who hollered at us about fatal threats, we didn't survive.

Our passengers speak in extremes, because that's how they alerted us to the prowling saber-toothed tiger. But our circulatory systems and nervous systems don't know the difference between the tiger problem and the algebra problem. After all, your passenger is shouting, *If you miss this algebra problem, you won't get into school, which means you won't get the job you want, which means you won't meet your spouse, which means you won't have a family, which means you won't be happy . . . .*

Our bodies take that kind of message literally. Thousands of years ago, no family or livelihood meant death. So our bodies do what they know how to do best, in order to stay alive: fight, flight, or freeze. In all three of these cases, the higher-thinking parts of our brain get robbed. Resources such as oxygen and sugar are shunted elsewhere. Our hearts start beating faster, getting ready for battle. Our muscles buzz with electricity.

When your anxious mind doesn't want to concentrate on some reading comprehension passage about algae blooms in the Gulf of Mexico, nothing is wrong with you. To the contrary, everything's acting exactly as it should. Your mind and body assume that the passengers are right, that your life is in danger. It's totally normal for passengers to make us anxious. This cause-and-effect link between passengers and anxiety is operating correctly.

Earlier in this chapter, I described the process of noticing, naming, engaging with, and welcoming passengers. But I'd like to underline a crucial moment—the moment when we recognize that passenger. It's just like the moment when we recognize whether we got an algebra problem right or wrong. When we recognize a passenger, it's easy to have a negative reaction. We can blame ourselves for the presence of the passenger. We can wish that the passenger weren't there. But that's just another way of wishing we were different. Under no circumstances should we blame ourselves for the presence of a passenger. We should never feel bad about our body's natural responses to passengers. When we recognize a passenger, that's *good* news. Remember how I celebrated when Bridget's passenger showed up? The presence of a passenger is a uniquely powerful opportunity to learn and address our unhelpful patterns. Each moment that we recognize a passenger should be a moment of celebration.

A Conversation with Chris

Chris is a friend and colleague who helped edit this book. During a brainstorming session at his house in North Carolina, he picked my brain on the concept of passengers.

Chris: So you're saying that my mind is like a car. And I have passengers in it. And those passengers are talking to me.

Me: It doesn't have to be a vehicle, but sure, a car is one thing you could imagine. And you could imagine this car not having lockable doors. You don't quite know who and when and how many passengers you're going to have.

Chris: So we have some frequenters, and some people who don't show up too often.

Me: Yes.

Chris: And you're saying I have to live with these people?

Me: I'm saying you already *are* living with them. The only thing I'm offering to change is your awareness of them and your relationship with them.

Chris: I'm a little terrified to know that there are other people in my head, and if I start listening to these voices too much, am I in danger of going crazy? Like, hey, which of my particular personalities is running things? Are they all going to bum rush the show and start driving?

Me: Remember, this is already happening. What I'm doing is offering a way to categorize and relate to those experiences to best serve our goals. It's actually good news that the voice that says, *I suck* and *I'm never going to do this right* isn't the real you.

Chris: What do you mean by the "real me"? Aren't the passengers me?

Me: That's where the driver part of the metaphor comes in.

The Driver

You may be wondering why there aren't any overtly positive and uplifting passengers in the framework I've presented. There are probably infinite ways to frame the human experience. Within this construct of passengers, sure, maybe every type of thought and emotion could be represented by a passenger. But then who would the driver be?

I posit that the driver is the part of us that surfaces when we feel safe, confident, and loved. I maintain that a core part of all of us is compassionate, empathetic, humble, clear, loving, intuitive, curious, and connected. Our driver is always in the driver's seat, though it may not have its hands on the wheel.

Different people have different passengers. But our drivers are all fundamentally similar. It's like Tolstoy wrote in *Anna Karenina*: "Happy families are all alike; every unhappy family is unhappy in its own way." In their wisdom and compassion, our drivers are all alike. Unlike passengers, who come and go when they please, drivers are always present.

The wisdom of our drivers is not just intelligence. It's an intuition, an attunement, an understanding of the true cause and effect of things. For instance, the driver in you knows that while procrastinating right now feels good, it won't feel good later, when you're no closer to your goal and with less time to spare.

When I was in college at the University of Georgia, I joined the Big Brother Big Sister program as a mentor. I was paired with a third grader named KJ. He was very, very quiet. For two years, he didn't speak more than a few words to me at a time. But I kept visiting KJ even when I moved away from Athens. He attended schools where fights and drugs were commonplace. I said everything a Big Brother should say, warning KJ about getting involved in drugs or violence. I knew that he might be swayed by his peers at school and learn lessons the hard way, but he never was. Finally, when he was about sixteen, I asked him, "Why didn't you do any of those things I warned you about? I figured you might still try them." In his characteristically unassuming manner, KJ shrugged and said, "I don't know. I guess in the end they just don't lead to good things."

That was KJ's driver displaying the wisdom to hear the chatter and temptations of passengers and still make a clear decision, one that focused on his own true welfare and that of others.

Recognizing the Driver

As Stella said earlier, sometimes it's difficult to discern whether a voice is that of your passenger or driver. You can recognize the driver both by what it says and by how it makes you feel. What it says usually has a connotation of support, love, and pragmatism—like a loving grandparent on a rocking chair who knows the ways of life.

Still, it can sometimes be difficult to distinguish between your driver and a passenger based solely on the words you hear. My passengers can occasionally sound like the driver, because what they're saying can sometimes be interpreted as supportive. For example, let's say you've been studying for your test for several hours every day for a week. Your mind says, *You need a break!* Is that your passenger who is just bored? Or is that the driver, seeing you are getting burned out and need rest?

When the words aren't enough to discern, we can rely on our physical sensations. In the coming pages, I will teach you how to become more attuned to subtle body sensations. It may take some time to notice and recognize the physical echoes of our passengers and of our drivers. Think of it as seeing tracks of an animal in the snow. Every animal has different tracks. We might not directly see the animal, but we can identify that it is present.

With practice, you will each get to know the somewhat unique physiological thumbprints of your passengers and driver.

But in the meantime, if your body feels contracted or sinking, a passenger is likely present. If your body feels expansive and energized, the driver is likely present.

Meeting My Driver

A few years ago I attended a three-month silent retreat at the Insight Meditation Society in Barre, Massachusetts. Along with ninety other participants, I woke up every morning to practice sitting meditation, followed by walking meditation, followed by sitting meditation, followed by walking meditation, etc. Even the meals were spent in silence. The teachers at the retreat invited us to use every moment to practice being mindful of whatever was arising, moment by moment, in our minds and bodies.

About two weeks in, I was having a really hard time. I couldn't keep my thoughts and emotions straight. I was desperately trying to figure out how to work with a particular emotion I had. The emotion itself was painful, but my doubt about how to work with that emotion was incapacitating. *Should I feel this sadness in the body, or notice the thoughts? In what order? Should I widen my attention or narrow it? I've heard teacher X say to widen it in this situation, but teacher Y said to narrow it.*

It was then that I realized how much I habitually depend on distractions for relief from my passengers. I normally watch videos, read a book, or talk to someone when several passengers show up. But on retreat, none of those distractions were available. I just had to sit with what was happening. Every escape door I was used to was locked. I sat down on a bench, my face in my hands, dejected. The bell was about to ring, signaling another forty-five-minute meditation session, which might as well have been called a torture session at that point.

Then, quite unexpectedly, I heard a voice say, *You're okay.* But it wasn't coming from anyone else. It was coming from my own mind, my voice. But it was saying something different than I was used to. It was being supportive. It almost seemed like a mistake. Like my self-critic had accidentally said something nice. But the voice kept saying it. *You're okay. You're okay. You're okay.* It must have said it a hundred times.

The message sounded foreign, but hearing it felt like drinking water after being dehydrated for days. I was a little nervous asking, but I asked the voice who it was. It said, *I'm you, and I've gotcha.* I burst into tears. I had always looked outside myself for the validation that this voice, *me*, was giving me.

This voice was there to supportingly counter the passengers as they kept popping up. It kept unconditionally supporting me, understanding me. At one point I asked it, *How long are you going to be here?* It didn't hesitate responding, *Forever.* I can't quite describe the relief I felt in that moment. It was partly because I had discovered another ally in life, and that always feels good. And it was partly because I knew it was a renewable resource. It was within me.

Have you ever heard someone who loves you describe you to someone else? When I used to hear my mom or best friend describe me, it just didn't resonate. They would talk about how selfless or wise or compassionate or something that I was, and I just thought they were off base, or embellishing at the very least.

I had finally met that person (myself) for the first time. My driver had been available for other people for several years, offering wise and compassionate support. But it had never been available to me, until that day. I don't believe it would have come to my aid had I just engaged in my habitual avoidance behaviors in the face of discomfort. You may have heard the saying "the only way out is through." That was true in my case.

This book is not meant to be the advice of your driver. Rather, it's meant to help you get in touch with your driver, so that you can access all the wisdom you need. I don't know when you need to study more or less, when you need to narrow or widen your perspective, or when you need to take a break or push through. Neither does anyone else.

Ever notice that for lots of timeless pieces of advice, there's an equal and opposite piece? "Absence makes the heart grow fonder" versus "out of sight, out of mind," for example. These kinds of contradictions are abundant in mindfulness and psychology, too. That's what I was wrestling with on the bench. I didn't know which suggestions to follow. But as you connect with your driver, that core part of you that's wiser than you realize, you'll cut out the noise. You'll be left with a few clear notes, such as I heard that day: *You're okay. I'm you. I gotcha. I'm here forever.*

Perhaps you've met your driver, perhaps not. Perhaps you'd like your driver to be more available to you. The good news is that we can actively cultivate the conditions for the driver to surface. I call it Driver's Ed, and there's a chapter on it later in this book. First, let's look at a few of the common passengers that surface and how drivers can interact with them.

Passenger Profiles

The passengers below are some of my own. They also frequent the minds of several people I know. I've described each passenger's typical activity, its common emotional and physical signs, and its good intention. I've also indicated how one might thank that passenger when it shows up, as well as how the driver might counter the passenger's message.

You'll see that these passengers overlap in various ways and are not mutually exclusive. As you consider how these passengers might show up for you during test prep or elsewhere in your life, and how you might deal with them, focus on the characteristics that are resonant and memorable to you.

Told Ya So

Activity: Told Ya So is the annoying friend or sibling who is always there to tell you, *I told you so* any time you fail. Told Ya So is the gloating voice of self-doubt after any performance. Told Ya So can list all the reasons it knew you were going to bomb.

Told Ya So is silent when you do well. If you get your goal score on a practice test, for example, you won't hear from Told Ya So. But if you score anywhere below your goal on a practice test, Told Ya So will be right there.

Told Ya So may also act like an overprotective parent, trying to justify that overprotectiveness. Imagine wanting to take the training wheels off your bike, but your parent doesn't want you to. You end up falling and scraping your knee. Your parent shakes his or her head, saying, "I told you so."

Emotional signs: Feeling sad and discouraged; feeling shame; feeling guilty.

Physical signs: Feeling lethargic, or as if your body is shrinking away; hanging your head.

Good intention underneath: Told Ya So actually cares about your well-being. Told Ya So knows how badly it hurts when you fail. Told Ya So's intention is not to make you feel bad but to keep you from going out on a limb in the future to prevent you from falling.

How to thank: *Thank you for trying to protect me.*

Driver's counter: *I know that it hurts when I fail. You're right about that. It's important for me to reflect and see if I actually did make a foolish decision in trying something. But in most cases the pain is temporary, such as when I perform poorly on a test. Those failures are not only inevitable but even necessary on my road to success. I need these failures. I still need you to keep me in line after doing something foolish, like jumping out of a plane without a reserve chute. But I don't need you to protect me from painful, yet survivable and character-building events, such as trying stand-up comedy and getting booed off stage.*

Compare Bear

Activity: Compare Bear ruthlessly compares you to other people. Sometimes Compare Bear tells you that you're outperforming others. This can cause you to feel better about yourself, but in a temporary, hollow way. Sometimes Compare

Bear tells you that you are *under*performing others, causing you to feel inadequate.

Compare Bear loves to make everything a competition. When I'm at the gym, Compare Bear peeks at the person next to me. *Is she running faster than me? Is he lifting more than me? When I'm studying, Compare Bear fantasizes that another student would be doing a better job with the problem in front of me.*

Compare Bear says things like this: *They're better than you. You're not good enough. You are way better than them. What do you think so-and-so would do in this situation? You don't measure up. People like other people more than they like you. Other people are _____er than you.*

Emotional signs: Feeling jealous, afraid, and anxious; feeling guarded.

Physical signs: Sometimes feeling inflated and powerful, for brief moments, when I'm being compared to someone I am outperforming. But most of the time, I feel tense, jittery, and small, as if I'm about to have to fight off a looming enemy.

Good intention underneath: Compare Bear ultimately wants you to belong. It doesn't want you to be excluded from the group.

It taps into a deep evolutionary need. Compare Bear knows that thousands of years ago, being exiled from the tribe meant death. It wants you to feel safe, in community with others.

How to thank: *Thank you for wanting me to belong.*

Driver's counter: *I will never be better than everybody in the world at anything. There will always be people who perform better and people who perform worse than I do. I have shown an ability in the past to do well at certain things. Doing worse than someone on some measure doesn't mean I will be outcast or ostracized. Whenever you show up, I will recognize you and* *hear you. But I may not always take your advice or believe everything you say.*

Later Gator

Activity: In short, Later Gator tells you to procrastinate. *You can wait till later. You deserve a break. This is so hard for you to do right now. Other stuff is more important right now. You need a quick nap, a bite, a walk, coffee.*

Later Gator uses any number of justifications to tell you not to do something right now. Most of these justifications are nonsense, but Later Gator is quite good with words. *You worked hard enough yesterday. You should call that friend, because isn't friendship more important than algebra rules? If you don't prioritize family and friends, then you're a bad person.*

Emotional signs: Feeling anxious and afraid, especially because the underlying tasks don't go away, nor does the pressure they produce.

Physical signs: Feeling tense and uneasy.

Good intention underneath: To prevent you from experiencing whatever negative emotions arise when you finally face the task that needs to be completed.

How to thank: *Thank you for wanting to keep me away from an unwanted experience.*

Driver's counter: *I know you want to keep me from doing this task to protect me from a negative experience. Thank you. But I need to face that negative experience head on, and I can do so. Avoidance hasn't helped me in the past.*

Imposter Pony

Activity: Imposter Pony tells you that you don't belong wherever you are. It thinks that you belong in a "lesser" crowd. Imposter Pony is there to knock you down a peg. *You don't deserve the role you're in. You don't deserve that award or those nice words. Just wait, because everyone's going to see you for who you really are.*

Emotional signs: Feeling anxious and trapped, even more so when good things are happening, because you think that the other shoe will drop any minute.

Physical signs: Feeling small; feeling tight in the chest, unable to breathe deeply; feeling tense.

Good intention underneath: Like a number of other passengers, Imposter Pony wants to protect you from harm. It doesn't want you to be rejected.

Imposter Pony also doesn't want you to get too prideful and arrogant. It doesn't want you to step out of line. As my dad used to say, it doesn't want you to "get too big for your britches."

How to thank: *Thank you for trying to protect me from getting in over my head. Thank you for trying to protect me from being rejected.*

Driver's counter: *I have many strengths and weaknesses, as do other people. Having weaknesses doesn't mean that I don't belong. It means that I'm human. I don't really know that other people are looking down on me. In fact, several people could be looking up to me right now.*

DisCount

Activity: DisCount always discounts your accomplishments. It shows up when things go well for you. It assigns the reason for your successes to something other than your own skill and talent. *You just got lucky when you got that problem right. Everyone has successes every now and then. You can't repeat that success.*

DisCount undercuts your strength. It saps your motivation by interrupting any momentum you build.

Emotional signs: Feeling discouraged and frustrated.

Physical signs: Feeling small and lethargic.

Good intention underneath: To protect you from future failure. By telling you that your accomplishment was luck, it discourages you from sticking your neck out in the future. It also wants to protect you from false pride and egotism.

How to thank: *Thank you for trying to keep me from having delusions of grandeur and from thinking that I am invincible.*

Driver's counter: *I'm in no danger of having too high of a self-esteem about my successes. In fact, I need a little more self-support, not less. So you don't have to spend so much energy discounting my accomplishments.*

Leap Frog

Activity: Leap Frog draws dramatic and catastrophic conclusions from the tiniest shreds of evidence. Miss a practice problem? *You will fail the test.* Get a bad test score? *You will never get into any school.* Confused about an explanation? *You don't understand math at all.*

Emotional signs: Feeling hypervigilant, on edge.

Physical signs: Feeling jittery and tight.

Good intention underneath: To protect you, as many other passengers do, from pain in the future. Leap Frog wants to spot that kind of pain and head it off early.

How to thank: *Thank you for looking out for me by watching for potential threats on the horizon.*

Driver's counter: *I understand that you want to be vigilant, and that you think you're being a realist about things. Sometimes the negative signs you focus on deserve that amount of attention. But not always. And in this case, right now, you are seeing things through a pessimistic lens. That's not necessarily reality.*

Knot Enough

Activity: Knot Enough says that you're inadequate. It's the quiet ringleader, and often one of our oldest and strongest passengers. *You're not worthy of success. You're not worthy of love. No one will hire you. No one wants to be with you.*

Knot Enough casts a deep, subtle, amorphous doubt over your value and ability. It whispers convincingly. Knot Enough sets you up for failure, and then Told Ya So confirms it later. Knot Enough believes that if you spread your wings, you still won't be able to fly.

Despite its negative messages, Knot Enough can be mistaken for the driver. Why? Because it's often present behind the scenes, and it might have been around for as long as you can remember.

Someone important to your survival may have told you as a very young child that something about you wasn't okay. Maybe that person meant that some of your behavior wasn't okay, but you heard it and internalized it as part of *you* isn't okay.

Emotional signs: Feeling sad, vulnerable, hopeless.

Physical signs: Feeling drained, weak.

Good intention underneath: Knot Enough tears you down before anyone else can. By its logic, the tearing down is inevitable, so it wants to do it in a more predictable and less negative way.

How to thank: *Thank you for trying to protect me from unpredictable pain.*

Driver's counter: *I know you tried to protect me so hard for so long. Now that I'm older and stronger myself, I can handle the periodic pain and rejection and failure that are a natural part of life. I couldn't as a kid, when I actually did need you.*

A Conversation with Alessandro

While no one is free of passengers, some people seem to experience them less. And some people naturally have a healthier relationship with the passengers that do arrive.

Despite fumbling on several problems that many of his classmates understand, my student Alessandro shows remarkable resilience and positivity. He bounces back, over and over again.

I decided to ask him about his approach to the test. Here is part of our conversation. As you can see, Alessandro expressed every skill, orientation, and technique that we are working on in this book.

Me: Many students beat themselves up when they miss an easy problem. Why don't you?

Alessandro: What if your best friend missed a problem? Would you yell at him? You've gotta be your own best friend, man.

Me: Why?

Alessandro: What's it going to help if you start being mean to yourself? Are you all of a sudden going to understand the problem? No way.

Me: What about all the immense pressure of the test? Lots of people feel overwhelmed, like the weight of the world is on their shoulders. Do you ever feel that?

Alessandro: No.

Me: Why not?

Alessandro: Because it doesn't matter.

Me: But doesn't it determine what school people get into, which determines what job they get, which determines what life they'll have, which determines if they'll ever be happy?

Alessandro: Well, yeah, kind of. Look at it this way: There's a difference between something being important and something being serious. Everything can't be serious. So it matters, but it doesn't matter.

Me: Don't you get frustrated when you don't get the practice scores you want?

Alessandro: A little, but the process is fun.

Me: Fun?

Alessandro: Yeah, think about it. These really smart people wrote a really smart test that teaches you and measures how well you can think in a certain way. Of course, it's not the only way to think or measure intelligence, but it's one way. It's debatable if this should be used to measure our aptitudes, but in the meantime, I get to learn a new way to think, and that's cool. Everybody has strengths and weaknesses in different areas. It just so happens that I don't have as much experience in this area as some other people.

Me: You didn't say, "I'm not as good" or "I can't be as good." You said, "I just haven't learned it." You didn't blame yourself.

Alessandro: Yeah, why would I? When I get all busy in my mind, I just have to take a deep breath and ground a little bit.

As you can imagine, Alessandro is improving much faster than he would if he were fettered by self-criticism and shame. Cases like Alessandro's prove that hope and despair are not the products of facts and events themselves. They are the products of our interpretations of facts or of our relationships to events. The math problem itself never causes despair or gives hope.

So what about the rest of us who tend to have pretty much the opposite reaction to adversity as Alessandro? Is there hope for us?

There's a concept called neuroplasticity, which basically means that the brain can structurally change with repeated activity. Your beliefs about the possibility of this change matter very much, too. Researcher Carol Dweck and others have run studies to show that if you adopt a "growth mindset" about your intelligence—that is, if you believe your intelligence can actually improve, if you believe you can actually get smarter— then it's more likely that you will actually get smarter.

But before we can form effective plans to work with and change our minds, we need to first recognize our current habits. That's why we need mindfulness.

CHAPTER 3

Mindfulness

Why Mindfulness?

I recently spoke with Dr. Rick Hanson, psychologist and author of *Hardwiring Happiness*, and I asked him how important mindfulness is for peak performance. He said, "It's essential. Without some type of metacognition about what is actually happening in our experience, we are on autopilot." Dr. Hanson's reasoning is predicated on the fact that our autopilots are often not tuned to perfection. On autopilot, we become puppets to our most deeply ingrained habits and patterns. In other words, our passengers take the wheel.

To do any real work with passengers, we have to reliably recognize them and their telltale signs. But getting to a point of reliable recognition is not easy. We have to bridge the gap between theory and practice—between reading about this stuff and actually doing it.

The Greek lyrical poet Archilochus wrote, "We don't rise to the level of our expectations, we fall to the level of our training." Champion boxer Mike Tyson said, "Everyone has a plan till they get punched in the mouth."

If you haven't been practicing mindfulness, then it's going to be difficult to use it when you're particularly stressed. That's why practicing mindfulness ahead of time, in more controlled scenarios, is beneficial.

You can think of studying, taking practice tests, and the real test as three increasingly difficult scenarios during which to practice mindfulness. Starting your mindfulness training during the test would be like practicing a new guitar solo in front of a sold-out crowd at a concert.

On one meditation retreat, I had somewhat of a mind-blowing realization. My mind was obsessing about practicing mindfulness perfectly. I thought it was a justified concern. After all, I was there to learn how to practice mindfulness. Then I remembered something I once heard a mindfulness teacher say: "How we handle this moment is the best predictor of how we will handle the next one."

Every stressful moment between now and your test is a gift. It's a crucial opportunity to notice what is arising in your mind and relate to it with acceptance, so you can be more prepared for test day. It's transformative to reframe the experience of stress as something to celebrate and take advantage of, rather than dread. We'll talk more about reframing later.

Even if you believe mindfulness is beneficial, you may think, *I don't have the luxury to be able to spend ten, twenty, thirty minutes per day just practicing mindfulness. I've got to learn a whole bunch of math. Every minute I spend practicing mindfulness is another minute I'm not doing things I need to do, such as study!*

It's an important concern. But do you have the same one about sleeping? Eating? Exercising? We all have to decide just how much time we should spend engaging in life- and body-sustaining activities. Thanks to an abundance of research and to our own experiences, few of us sacrifice all sleep and exercise time. We know that without them, we would perform worse at just about everything. In some sense, we can think of mindfulness practice just as we do physical exercise: it conditions and trains a part of us to perform optimally.

Let's make this more tangible. Assume that you have ten free hours per week. How much of that should you spend studying and how much of it should you spend practicing mindfulness? You should definitely spend more than zero minutes practicing mindfulness. But more than one hour? I don't know. More than two? Probably not. It's worth exploring on your own.

Stimulus and Response

Our bodies and minds have an amazing, innate ability to optimize themselves, if we just let them. Sometimes, all we have to do is notice what's going on. Scientists continue to experiment with processes called biofeedback and neurofeedback, by which a person connected to electrical monitors sees real-time representations of his or her heart rate, blood pressure, and other bodily and mental activities.

It turns out that when a person using biofeedback sees a monitor displaying the overactivation of the nervous system, the system often starts to correct itself on its own, without voluntary effort.

Do you remember the exercise in which I had you notice tense areas of your body? Often, when your attention lands on a place of tension, that tension releases spontaneously. Likewise, simply bringing attention to certain kinds of mental or physical issues can be enough to remedy them. Sometimes, though, we need to do more. We may need to invoke choice.

In his best-selling book *Man's Search for Meaning*, the pioneering physician, therapist, and Holocaust survivor Viktor Frankl wrote, "Between stimulus and response there is space. In that space is our power to choose." When unmindful, that space often goes unnoticed. For example, it may seem as if there's no time or space between glancing at a probability problem and your heart starting to race. It may seem as if there's no gap between seeing the face of an ex-friend and feeling deep anger or sadness.

Mindfulness highlights the space, and can even seem to slow down time a little, creating the useful illusion of having more opportunity to make choices. Just as a high-powered microscope can reveal the monumental space between an electron and a proton, you can learn to perceive, through mindfulness, the gaps between events in a sequence.

Marvel Comics superhero Quicksilver moves so fast that he can experience time as if everything else is in slow, almost frozen motion. In one scene in an X-Men movie, he runs around a room disarming the bad guys before anyone has time to blink. Mindfulness lets us experience life more like Quicksilver.

Breaking the Chain

About three years ago, I had an argument with my best friend about a betrayal. The argument was tense and largely unproductive. In the weeks and even months afterward, I found myself spinning, analyzing, and investigating that argument from every angle. I repeatedly felt every emotion and watched my mental and emotional patterns.

It's useful to see patterns, as long as they offer us information. But once we see and understand the patterns clearly, digging and analyzing rarely helps. One of my mindfulness teachers said such digging was like a dog chewing on a dry bone. Sometimes there's just nothing left.

I'm guessing that many of the stories you have found, or will find, that frequent you the most during test prep have a familiar course to them—a familiar starting place, familiar emotions, a familiar ending place. Once you really know the pattern, you can give yourself permission to just disengage as soon as you recognize any part of its life cycle. It's important not to disengage from a place of anger, but from a place of wisdom. Rather than *I hate thinking about this, so I'm going to block it out of my mind,* you can think *I've thought about this from most angles and letting this go would be best.*

The story will likely reappear, just due to habit. That's okay. Just keep practicing letting it go.

What Is Mindfulness?

Mindfulness can sometimes be easily defined as the opposite of mindlessness. Have you ever been in a movie theater, completely engrossed in the movie—so much so that you've lost all awareness about "the real world"? You aren't thinking about your friends, family, or job, because you're so invested in the plight of the heroine. Then you hear the people behind you in the theater talking. You're immediately zapped out of your movie trance and back into the real world.

Our thoughts can be just as engrossing as movies, complete with complex characters, soundtracks, vivid images, and captivating plot twists. It's not a problem to get lost in thought, just as it's not a problem to get lost in a movie. But it *is* a problem if it happens for too long without us knowing it. We can call that mindlessness—being lost in a fantasy thought world, detached from the happenings of the here and now.

But as soon as you are consciously *aware* that you are watching a movie, you're no longer absorbed in the movie. You're present. Similarly, as soon as you're *aware* that you're thinking, you're already back in the present moment. You're being mindful.

The words *present moment* are associated with mindfulness because, technically, all that is ever happening is happening right now. Yes, there was a yesterday. Presumably, there will be a tomorrow as well. But it is also true that yesterday and tomorrow are just figments of our imagination. In a sense, they aren't real. Henry David Thoreau wrote of living in the present in this way: ". . . to stand on the meeting of two eternities, the past and future, which is precisely the present moment; to toe that line."

Toeing that line takes practice, because both eternities contain an infinite number of seductive stories.

Finding the Present

Bring to mind the last conversation you had. Allow the memories of the person, the words, and the feelings to permeate your awareness.

Now imagine contacting that person again and asking them whate their favorite food is. Imagine that scenario, including their potential response.

You have just found the past and the future. Now see if you can find the present.

The breath is a perpetual portal to the present moment. It's always happening, and it's always now. Take a moment to let your awareness locate sensations of your breath, either at the nostrils or at the belly.

See if you can be in the present with your breath. Imagine that the zero on a number line represents the present moment, the negative numbers represent the past, and the positive numbers represent the future. Be on the zero with the sensations of your breath.

As you zoom in toward zero, you may find that you can't be with the entire length of the breath in the present moment, because the breath lasts longer than a moment. In fact, you can't be with one in-breath in this moment, because the in-breath lasts longer than a moment. On the number line, it's not a point but a splat around zero, stretching into the positive and the negative numbers (or past and future).

In truth, you can only be with this instant, this fraction of the breath. Right now. And right now. And right now. Toe that line.

Most thoughts are about the past or future, or interpretations about the present moment. In other words, if we are thinking, we are likely not present. It's not bad to think. Thinking is great. The problem occurs when we spend too much time in our thoughts and when we believe them.

So we need to practice living in the present and practice noticing when we are in mental movies. That's what mindfulness is—recognizing and accepting what is actually happening right now in our experience, in a nonjudgmental way.

Notice that I did not say, "Have fewer thoughts" or "Be calmer." Those are probably two of the most perpetuated, misguided, and harmful myths about mindfulness. While it is true that fewer thoughts and less anxiety can be byproducts of mindful practice, they are not necessary to practice mindfulness. One can be just as mindful of a quiet mind as a busy mind. One can be just as mindful of a calm body as a jittery one.

Mindfulness is not clearing your mind or being calmer. Mindfulness is noticing and accepting whatever you experience. That's it. It's not complicated, but it's also not always easy.

Only Six Things

There are infinite different sensory experiences and infinite ways to categorize those experiences. So let's bucket our experiences into the following six categories: touch, sight, taste, smell, sound, and thought. Can you find anything in your current experience that couldn't be included in the above categories? Search for a moment before reading on.

This is not the only way to categorize our experiences, but it is *a* way. Subscribing to these categories makes understanding our experiences more digestible and more manageable.

Here's everything I'm experiencing right now: Breeze on skin (touch). Sound of music in headphones (sound). Feeling of breath through nose (touch). Feeling of computer keys on my fingers (touch). Searching for something else to notice (thought). Wondering if I'm doing this right (thought). Feeling of happiness (touch and/or thought). Feeling my mouth smiling (touch). Wondering what you will think of reading this (thought). Smell of the trees and flowers in my backyard (smell).

Now you try.

EXERCISE

Six Senses

Find a comfortable place to sit, stand, walk, or lie down. Your posture doesn't really matter. Turn your phone on airplane mode. Give yourself permission to step away from every project for the next five minutes.

When I name the following things, see if your awareness naturally notices them.

The sensation of the breath going in and out of the nostrils . . . tension in the neck or shoulders . . . sounds of the room or space . . . the mind wondering . . . the mind having thoughts about this very exercise . . . the smell of some fragrance.

You can play with your awareness like this, directing the different experiences on purpose for a minute.

Now let go of all intentional direction of your awareness. Practice just noting what arises. Begin by asking yourself, *What am I aware of?*

There's no wrong or right answer here. You're experiencing *something,* even if that experience is trying to find what you're experiencing. If this is the case, you would just label "thought" or "touch," depending on how you experience trying to find something.

But you really don't have to try to find experiences. They just arrive in your awareness. This can be a helpful exercise when you are experiencing overwhelm. If you find something that you don't think belongs in the six categories above, make yourself a new category! The point is to be able to categorize and simplify your experiences.

Pedestrians

The better we get at noticing our thoughts, the better we get at noticing our passengers. After all, our passengers are just recurring patterns of thoughts and emotions.

But most thoughts don't qualify as passengers. Most thoughts are just random and unobtrusive. Yet, they still occupy significant airtime in our consciousness, especially when we engage with them. Continuing with the passenger/driver metaphor, we can call our random and fleeting thoughts *pedestrians*. Pedestrians don't require our attention or engagement, as passengers often do. Pedestrians aren't in the car with us, so they aren't as distracting as passengers. If we just notice them and keep driving, they disappear in the rearview mirror.

If we don't notice them, however, we can end up thinking about their messages for a surprising amount of time. If you've ever caught yourself daydreaming in class or at work, you were probably listening to pedestrians, who can mentally take us to some weird places. If I tune into my pedestrians in this moment, here is the chatter I hear:

I wonder how many bicycles there are in the world. Probably a lot. Do most people know how to ride bikes? What if bikes could fly? That would be cool. What if I could fly? I wonder if flies know they can fly. If a fly is flying inside an airplane, does that airplane weigh more? I bet people from 200 years ago would be really freaked out by airplanes.

Sometimes you'll see the same pedestrians several times within a mindfulness practice, or throughout your day. Pedestrians are always subcategories of the six sense experiences we've identified. If a pedestrian is persistent enough, it's okay to give it a name, rather than just labeling it one of the six sense categories. Giving it a more specific name can cause the pedestrian to subside quicker than it otherwise would. For example, if you stubbed your toe yesterday, and the throbbing keeps distracting you, it's okay to name that "toe" or "throbbing" when it hijacks your attention, rather than noting the sense category "touch."

When we don't notice a stimulus, it often turns into a story, carrying us into the past or future. And we get hooked.

A Line of Hooks

Over the past several years, Joseph Goldstein—author and cofounder of the Insight Meditation Society in Barre, Massachusetts—has been my primary mindfulness teacher. He is widely regarded as one of the kindest and wisest mindfulness teachers in the West. In the coming pages, I will be sharing some our conversations with you, just referring to him as Joseph.

He once described the constant inflow of sensory data as a line of hooks slowly moving by us. Seductive thoughts dangle in front of us like worms in front of a fish. If we grab onto one of those hooks, we get taken for a ride into a cascade of multiplying thoughts. We often don't even realize that we're hooked. Have you ever been going about your day only to "wake up" in the middle of an imagined scenario in your mind? Arguing with someone, bombing a test, fighting off an army of stuffed unicorns, whatever.

We can think of mindfulness practice as a continual exercise in unhooking. We can also think of unhooking as letting go. There is great relief in releasing a mental story. The body relaxes and the mind settles. And every time we drop a story, we strengthen our "letting-go muscles."

The mind reminds me of a crocodile's jaws. Crocs have the strongest bite ever recorded, at 3,700 pounds of force per square inch. It's virtually impossible to open their jaws once they clamp down on something. And yet, a small child can hold a croc's mouth shut with little effort, because the jaw-*opening* muscles are so weak.

Likewise, our minds can latch onto a story with impressive strength, ruminating and spinning for hours at a time. But we're not so good at opening our mental jaws, at unhooking ourselves.

A man who was born with the name Robert Jackman studied at the University of California, Berkeley, then traveled to Asia as a Peace Corps volunteer in the 1960s. He is now a senior monk and teacher known as Ajahn Sumedho. He recently said that, when he traveled to Asia, he had a mind prone to thinking and ruminating, grabbing every hook that dangled in front of him. To untrain that habit, his entire mindfulness practice for two years boiled down to two words: *let go*. Let go of every thought, every emotion, every impulse, even of the idea of letting go. Everything.

You don't have the luxury of living your life like that right now. You have a test to study for. But you can still practice letting go, deliberately and purposefully, every so often at selected times. This way, when you find yourself caught in mental stories woven by pedestrians or passengers—whether during your preparation, during the test itself, or at any other time—you can unhook yourself more easily.

EXERCISE

Letting Go

Think of the last meal you had. Imagine yourself in that situation, with the food in front of you. Remember the sight, smell, and taste of the food. Remember who or what was around you.

Now drop that story, and let your awareness land on something in the present. A sensation, a sound, anything.

Acknowledge that space between letting one story go and your awareness landing on another experience. That infinite, free-floating space.

Repeat—think of something, intentionally hooking yourself. Then intentionally let go. Notice the sensation of letting go. Notice the space between letting go and returning to the present. Notice the present.

Repeat.

Perpetual Push and Pull

Every time we experience a sensory input, we have one of three orientations to it. We like it, don't like it, or don't really care. There's no problem with any of these orientations. The problem occurs when we automatically react to our orientations, specifically the liking and disliking.

When we like something, we try to get more of it. We get a dopamine rush when we experience something pleasant, so we equate that rush with happiness. We can begin to seek out pleasure at every turn. That's one way addiction happens. People can be addicted to all sorts of things: success, popularity, social media, or even self-criticism.

Think back on your own life and any big pursuits you've had. Maybe to be a good athlete, to be popular, to be a good student, to be a good family member, to make money? I'm sure you have experienced at least momentary success in at least one of these categories. Was the happiness from any of those successes permanent? Of course not. Nothing is. We *think* we are chasing the thing itself (the money, popularity, grades, etc.), but we're not. We're chasing that brief feeling of elation we get when that thing happens. And we're deluding ourselves into thinking that feeling will last just a little longer next time. But there's never enough. Never enough money. Never enough popularity. Never enough A's.

When we *don't* like something, on the other hand, we try to avoid it. That's helpful when what we don't like is an actual threat to us, such as a toxic food or an abusive person. But we tend to spend a lot of time and energy avoiding things that are only slightly unpleasant and pose no threat to us— an intermittently annoying person, a slightly uncomfortable posture, the feeling of vulnerability. Every moment we spend avoiding something minor is a moment we could have spent doing something productive.

Freedom happens when we realize that our happiness is not dependent on the things we are chasing. We can then choose to pursue whatever we want, without the illusion that the object of pursuit will complete us, or permanently satisfy some deep need we have.

There's a scientific name for this phenomenon: "hedonic adaptation" or the "hedonic treadmill." Really good things that occur in your life make you really happy . . . for a while. Then you adapt, and you tend to revert to your normal level of happiness. Ask most lottery winners. Likewise, really bad occurrences make you really unhappy for a while, but you tend to recover more than you anticipate you will.

In a nutshell, we overestimate the impact of future events on our happiness, such as reaching some goal or achieving some dream.

I'm incredibly lucky to say that, by most modern measures of success, I can point to at least a brief time in my life when

I had it—owning a house, having an intimate relationship, getting into an Ivy League school, getting a good job, having friends, being financially comfortable, etc. But not one of these things delivered me lasting happiness. At best, I got a three- or four-week boost in mood. I suspected that my pursuits of fulfillment were slightly misguided, but I didn't know for sure until three and a half weeks into the three-month silent meditation retreat that I wrote about earlier.

Here is my journal entry from day twenty-four of that three-month retreat:

Everything has been taken away . . . everything that helps me avoid feeling unpleasant emotions. No video, no books, no conversation, no money, no job, no dating, no pets. At first, in this seeming void, you resist it and crave for the distractions you're used to. Then you see unpleasant reactions to not being able to satisfy your habits—anxiety, laziness, depression. All things that we've been conditioned to think are "bad" traits. But as you meditate, you realize that those things are not "you," that you can't control if they arise any more than you can control the weather. Then slowly, a compassionate voice begins to meet this newly uncovered suffering. This gives birth to a subtle strength and resilience. What naturally follows this brave and loving connection to one's own suffering, is compassion for the suffering of others. How amazing. It's bizarre to think that I'm just as happy as I've ever been, and I have none of the things that I have always thought I needed to be happy. But this process has to happen experientially, slowly, by watching our own mind and body, nonjudgmentally, moment after moment. I tried to "understand" my way to relief for almost ten years by reading dozens of books and talking to dozens of experts on mindfulness. Ironically, they all said that cognitive understanding wasn't enough . . . that I'd have to do the work. Some part of me thought that I could bypass that step for so long.

I'm not saying that pursuing money, success, popularity, relationships, or accolades is inherently misguided. I am pursuing all of those things right now. But I am saying that it's important to investigate the motivation for pursuing those things. Sometimes it's surprising what we find when we look at our motivation. Sometimes we have attached several goals to a certain task, hoping that the accomplishment of that task will take care of the rest of those issues—kind of like riders on a bill that have little or no connection to the subject matter.

Your performance on the test will only increase when you don't have the myth of everlasting happiness attached to it. Because this attachment puts the weight of the world on the test. No one can lift that much.

Things Change

Through the letting-go practice, we start to see that every experience just comes and goes. No matter how wonderful, no matter how terrible, it just comes and goes. And we don't have a choice. Remember the last wonderful thing that happened to you? How long did it last? What about the last terrible thing? Perhaps the memory of those things lasted, but did the actual event? Yet we spend so much of our time in denial of this basic fact, by trying to hold on to and continue good experiences and to prevent bad ones.

I'm not saying we don't have any control in our lives. I'm saying we significantly overestimate the amount of control that we do have. This overestimation, paradoxically, keeps us enslaved to whatever random arisings of sensory data that occur. We react, react, react. But there's another option. Just watch. Watch the mind with the kindness, dispassion, and perspective of that loving grandparent.

Letting go is another way of stopping the feeding of experience. Left to their own devices, experiences will arise and pass away in a matter of seconds. We are the ones who fan the flames of various thoughts and emotions. Have you noticed how sounds just come and go, regardless of our agenda? Before reading on, try to make any sound that is happening right now become permanent.

Our emotions and thoughts have the same transience as sound, if we don't feed them. Before reading on, reflect on how a deep understanding of this inevitable transience could be beneficial to you.

Check Your Motivation

Everyone takes standardized tests, but not for the same reasons. The standardized test journey is a long and arduous one, and if you aren't in touch with your motivation for taking it, you may run out of steam along the way. I was surprised to learn that many of my students aren't even aware of their motivation. One of my students discovered that her motivation stemmed from her desire to impress her mother. Another found that he really just wanted to feel smart around his peers. Yet another, named Avni, discovered that she just wanted to be happy, and she had subconsciously decided that the test would deliver that happiness.

Avni was extremely nervous when we were working together. She was studying for the GMAT, trying to get into business school. She's very bright but just couldn't seem to focus or perform well. In an attempt to figure out the root of her anxiety and poor performance, I wanted to find her true motivation for studying. So, during one of our tutoring sessions, I asked her why she was nervous about the problem in front of her. She said that if she didn't do well on the problem, she wouldn't do well on the test. I asked her why that mattered. She said that she then wouldn't get into business school. I asked her why that mattered. She said that she then wouldn't meet her husband. That meant she would never have kids. And that meant that she would never be happy.

She had attached so many deep wants and needs of hers to the test, weighing it down so much that it would be impossible for anyone to lift. I asked her, "Are you even interested in business?" She seemed surprised by the question. She had never really thought about it. It turns out that she had no interest in business. After exploring her actual passions, we discovered her interests lie in health care, specifically in caring for the elderly. Avni is now pursuing her master's degree in public health.

How many life paths would be different if people paused, looked beneath the fear, and asked themselves what they really wanted? Avni had let fear drive her decisions. When she connected with her deepest motivation, she connected with her inspiration. Driven by inspiration, rather than fear, her test prep performance improved dramatically.

Painted Tiger

A Bengali meditation teacher called Munindraji—who taught many prominent American teachers, including Sharon Salzberg, Surya Das, and Joseph Goldstein—once said, "The thought of your mother is not your mother."

We tend to conflate the *content* of our thoughts with some objective reality. For example, if a student has the thought *I am bad at math*, the student rarely questions it as anything other than a true depiction of who the student is.

There is a world of difference between *I am bad at math* and *I notice the thought that I am bad at math.* Following *I am* with any descriptor reduces us to a static fixture of that descriptor. But saying *I notice* allows perspective and implicitly acknowledges that we are more than whatever it is that we are noticing in any given moment. You can incorporate this perspective into your experience with this subtle shift in terminology:

I am going to fail → *I notice* the thought that I am going to fail.

I am worried → *I notice* thoughts about the future.

I am nervous → *I notice* an increased heart rate and tingling in my stomach.

Reframing our experiences from *I am* to *I notice* desolidifies and depersonalizes our experiences, thereby inducing a sense of perspective and freedom. But this reframing isn't a magic pill. Sometimes we can intellectually know that our thoughts aren't objective physical symptoms, such as faster heart rate, sweaty palms, clenched jaw, jittery feelings, etc.

To illustrate this point, many meditation teachers share the following allegory. A thousand years ago, a master artist was commissioned to paint a large mural of a tiger. The artist was superstitious about looking at his paintings before completion, so he would cover various parts of the canvas as he worked, so as never to see the creation until completion. After several weeks, he painted the final stroke and allowed himself to remove the cover and step back and view his creation. Before he knew it, he was running away in fear. The painting had looked so realistic that, even though he intellectually knew he was only looking at paint and canvas, his body thought it was a real tiger.

Whenever you find yourself repeatedly physically reacting to the story of a future event, such as a standardized test, you can label that story *Painted Tiger*. This will help remind your brain, and your body, that what you're reacting to is a fantasy of your own creation. You could even make Painted Tiger one of your passengers.

Dropping the "I"

One further level of freedom, beyond changing *I am* to *I notice*, is dropping the *I* altogether.

Here are a few examples of how to change *I notice* to *There is:*

I notice the thought that I can't do this → *There is* thinking about failure.

I notice thoughts about the future → *There is* thinking about the future.

I notice an increased heart rate and tingling in my stomach → *There is* an increased heart rate and tingling in the stomach.

By doing dropping the *I*, we are taking the subject out of the experience, thereby loosening the stickiness of the self, which can have a lot of baggage. Anytime we involve *my* or *I*, we involve all of our associations with the self. Bringing context to momentary noticings is sometimes useful, but it often just muddies our experience with biases and judgments. That's why *There is anxiety* is slightly less likely to prompt self-criticism than *I notice anxiety*, which is slightly less likely to prompt self-criticism than *I am anxious*.

But before we get ahead of ourselves, we have to actually *notice* our thoughts before we can begin to separate ourselves from them.

Noticing

In modern society we are so inundated with sensory data that we don't usually have a choice about what we're going to notice. Billboards, storefronts, television stations, and smartphone apps fight for who can be the most interesting, trying to be the loudest and brightest. Our attention acts like a puppy, lunging from one treat to the next with reckless abandon.

By looking at the shiniest thing in front of us, we turn a blind eye to the second most enticing thing in our experience, or the third—which may actually be more important than the first.

You can think of our current life experience at any given moment as an orchestra of activity. We're just used to paying attention to the loudest, most obvious, or most pleasurable instrument. Let's say that you like to listen to piano. When you listen to an orchestra, it's easy for you to hear the piano. If you try, you can also hear the violins. But even if you concentrate really hard, you cannot hear the cellos underneath. And yet, you would certainly notice if the cellos were missing. Through mindfulness practice, I'm going to help you notice the cellos of your experience.

One useful way of noticing the cellos in an orchestra would be to silence the other instruments. Likewise, one way to notice subtler and subtler parts of our experience is to reduce stimulation. That's why mindfulness retreats often occur in quiet and serene circumstances. Limiting external stimuli, such as conversation and technology can make our internal experiences more apparent. It's not that our thoughts and emotions become more prominent in and of themselves; it's that everything else recedes.

In the children's book *Where's Waldo*, each page shows hundreds of people in very busy places, such as markets, streets, and fairs. One of those little cartoon people is a guy in a red-and-white-striped shirt, blue pants, and glasses. His name is Waldo. The reader's job is to find Waldo. Waldo would be much easier to find if there were fewer people in the market with him. In fact, with each person progressively removed, Waldo would become increasingly easier to spot, right?

Similarly, each part of our internal experience becomes easier to notice as external distractions diminish: The subtle tingling on the bottom of the right foot; the slight tension on the right side of the jaw; the subtle nagging worry that I haven't studied enough today.

Once you have spotted Waldo, it's easy to identify him again, even with all of the other people around. Likewise, once you've heard the cellos, it's easy to identify them again, even with all of the other instruments playing.

The more you practice noticing your experiences in a fairly low stimulus environment, the more you will be able to attend to them during stressful situations, such as studying for a standardized test.

Passenger Origins

In one of my recent test prep classes, I assigned the students a difficult problem to complete in a short amount of time. I told

told them to notice any limiting thoughts or emotions that came up while solving.

One student, Katie, said that she noticed her mind go cloudy. Several of the other students nodded in agreement.

A passenger has likely been present for several seconds or even minutes before we notice such gross symptoms as a cloudy mind. So I asked Katie what specific thoughts and beliefs accompanied and preceded cloudiness.

Emily, who had also nodded along with Katie's recount of symptoms, identified several hindering thoughts: *I'm not good at non-algebraic methods. I won't be able to get those. I'm not creative enough.*

I said, "So, you start doing a problem, and if you're challenged with trying something new that you're not comfortable with, you recognize that you can't do it in that moment. Then you say to yourself that you'll never be able to do it. Then you say you don't have the creativity or potential to do it. And that means you'll never change, never learn anything new, never amount to anything. Is that about right?"

As I spoke, Emily more and more enthusiastically nodded and smiled and eventually laughed. "Yes! Yes! I will never amount to anything!!"

Laughing is often a sign that we are no longer in the grip of our passengers. When we play out our passengers' logic to the end, the absurdity and extremity of the logic often causes us to smile.

Together, as a class, we named Emily's passenger. An acronym I use for non-algebraic methods is BEDS (backward, estimation, drawing, smart numbers). So one of the students said we should name Emily's passenger *Bedbug*.

Passengers tend to interfere in a series of escalating behaviors until they get our attention, much as people do. A passenger may show itself so subtly that you don't even notice at first. Then it may start speaking louder. Then it might hijack your nervous system and make you anxious. Then it might flood you with mental images. Passengers want to be heard and validated just like all of us do. It's never too late to hear and validate them. Through mindfulness practice, we can recognize passengers earlier and earlier in their visitations.

The sooner we notice the passenger, the sooner we can choose how to proceed. For example, when Emily observes the thought, *I'm not good at knowing how to break solutions*, she can follow it up with the word *yet*. Or she can look at the passenger and say, *Hey, I see you*. Seeing gives us choice. One way to train ourselves to see passengers sooner is to dedicate several minutes per day to the practice of watching thoughts and emotions arise in the present moment—mindfulness. The more we practice mindfulness, the more likely we are to catch passengers before they cause too much damage.

Even if we don't notice a passenger's presence until several steps down the road, when the mind has become cloudy, it's still helpful to retrace the passenger's steps. This way, we become intimately familiar with each step of each passenger's likely path, allowing us to identify passengers more easily and let go of their storylines with more confidence. As one of my students Troy recently said, "I noticed a voice telling me that I needed to plan my weekend, but I know that passenger and I know where it leads. So I just let it go."

EXERCISE

Seeing Things Arise

Find a comfortable seat, either in a chair or on a cushion. It's best to be upright, sitting fairly straight, but not rigid. Your hands can rest in your lap in any way that's comfortable. Remember that mindfulness practice is possible in any posture, so no need to worry too much about minute details here.

First, inhale slowly through your nose, feeling the air go all the way down to your pelvis, filling your belly and lower back. On the exhale through your mouth, feel all of your muscles letting go, as if they're melting. But keep an upright posture. Repeat this breath three times.

Allow your awareness to rest on the nostrils or upper lip. Notice what the movement of the breath feels like, without manipulating the breath. Pay attention to the breath as if you had never really noticed it before. Notice how the in-breath feels different than the out-breath. Notice the pauses between the breaths. Let your awareness look at your breath as a child would look at a new toy. Look at it from all sides with curiosity.

There's no need to analyze the breath intellectually or remember anything you discover about it. Just notice.

Allow the awareness to stay with the bare sensations of the air passing through your nose or over your lip. Just know you're breathing in and know you're breathing out.

If it helps, you can make mental note *in* on the in-breath and *out* on the out-breath, over and over. Rather than thinking of this exercise as trying to being aware for ten minutes straight, just be aware for the length of this breath. Then this breath. Then this one.

When the mind wanders, as it will, celebrate that you became aware of the wandering. Then, gently and slowly allow your attention to move back to the breath. In. Out. You can think of your attention as a pet you are walking that starts to walk into someone's garden. You want to guide your pet back onto the sidewalk, but don't want to jerk the leash too hard.

If you find yourself getting tense or frustrated, just repeat the three deep breaths at the beginning of this exercise.

Then return your attention to your nose or upper lip, and rest your awareness on the sensations of the breath.

Attention

The "Seeing Things Arise" exercise doubles as attention practice.

Just out of curiosity, while reading the past several pages, have you checked your phone? If you're reading online, have you checked another browser?

Attention is that faculty of mind that allows us to have our awareness on an object. For example, right now your attention is on the words that you're reading. But we seldom keep our attention on one thing for very long, partially due to the constant onslaught of sensory input by phones and other technology. Some people intentionally move their attention from one thing to another in rapid succession, calling it multitasking. Whether intentional or unintentional, breaking attention just trains the mind to break attention.

Being good at multitasking is a myth. As soon as you switch from one task to another—for example, from reading an email to solving a math problem—you incur something called a switching cost. A switching cost is a loss in efficiency that occurs because the mind needs to stop, reorient itself, and get back up to speed on each new task. It takes the mind more time and energy to start from zero and build momentum than to maintain it.

I recently watched a strongman competition in which each contestant had to pull an entire vehicle with a rope. It was obvious that the most difficult part of the task was starting from a standstill. Once the vehicle was rolling, the contestant could utilize the momentum already gained. Imagine if the contestants had to move two cars across the finish line, one at a time. The best strategy would be to pull one car along the track all the way to the finish, then turn to the second car. It would be very inefficient to pull one car for a few yards, then dash to the other car and pull it for a few yards, then dash back to the first car, etc. Each car would lose momentum and grind to a halt, and the contestant would have to keep starting over with each car from a dead stop.

When you bounce from composing one email to reading an article to checking social media, and back within a few minutes, you lose momentum.

But some tasks can be pretty boring. Is it any wonder that after four minutes of a reading comprehension passage, your mind says, *Uh, I'm bored. Let's think about something else now*? One of the benefits of mindfulness practice is that it trains our attention to rest on a certain object for a sustained period of time. We'll call that concentration. Researchers at the University of California, Santa Barbara conducted an experiment in which a group of test prep students practiced forty-five minutes of mindfulness, four times per week, for two weeks. Not only did their test scores increase by an average of 16 percent, but the section of the test that saw the most improvement was reading comprehension. The UCSB scientists concluded that cultivating mindfulness is an effective method for increasing cognitive function and reducing mind-wandering.

As I'm sure you've already realized, the mind naturally wanders. Sometimes my attention will wander for minutes at a time before remembering to come back to the breath. Then five seconds later, it will wander off again. But every one of those five seconds is training my attention. All you need is one moment of mindfulness to make an entire mindfulness practice worth it.

During a mindfulness retreat at Spirit Rock Meditation Center in California, one of the more experienced participants raised her hand to ask the teacher a question. "When I try to meditate, sometimes my mind wanders almost the whole time. How many times do I have to notice that my mind is wandering for it to be worth meditating at all?" The teacher didn't hesitate. She said, "Once." Once. That's all it takes for a mindfulness practice to be worth it. If your mind immediately starts wandering and you only catch it once, you've succeeded. Make that your bar of success. Once.

Enough Time for Mindfulness?

Some students really buy into the idea of passengers and mindfulness and say, "That all sounds great, Logan, but I don't have time to practice mindfulness outside of the test, let alone during the test when I'm being timed!"

So let's look at a real situation of how someone could use mindfulness successfully during a high-stress, time-pressured situation.

If you recall, my sister Maisie won the silver medal in the jiu-jitsu world championship this year. I was talking to her on the phone yesterday when she randomly said, "I wouldn't have won my first match if it weren't for your mindfulness stuff. That girl was choking me, and I just started practicing mindfulness."

I asked her how. She said, "I noticed a passenger saying, *Just give up. Just go to sleep.* But I *noticed* that it was just a passenger! So I wondered where the driver was. And I heard the driver say, *Breathe. Now try. You're not dead yet.* Anyway, it was a really cool moment, and I thought of you while I was being choked."

I said, "That all happened in the few seconds while she was choking you?" Maisie said, "Yep. It's the only reason I rallied and won the match."

I figure if she has time to practice mindfulness while her world is going dark, we can practice in pretty much any situation.

Acceptance

After a few months of mindfulness practice, one of my mindfulness students had an epiphany. "Fighting a thought is just fighting with yourself. It never works. If you're gonna try to egg on the bully, how often does that work? You just have to accept that the bully is in your social studies class. Get an A and move on."

Acceptance is an essential ingredient of mindfulness. If I notice that my stomach feels jittery during algebra, but I spend my energy wishing that this weren't the case, I'm fighting the present moment rather than living in it. The present moment is happening. Wishing that it weren't, or denying it, is nonsensical. It's like wishing that it weren't raining while it's raining. Or worse, denying that it's raining while it's raining. When we fight with reality, we lose.

The most common pushback I hear from students is, "How will I ever improve if I just stay complacent with the way things are?" They think that acceptance equates to future resignation. But accepting that this moment is happening doesn't preclude us from trying to shape the next moment. If you want to change a habit or a behavior or a situation, it's even more important to accept the way it is at the moment. We always have to start from where we are.

Another reason to cultivate acceptance is that, paradoxically, it makes unpleasant situations more bearable. One study done at Leeds Beckett University in the UK lends support to this. Two groups were instructed to place their hands in buckets of ice water. One group was given mindfulness instructions, and the other wasn't. The group that heard mindfulness instructions reported less pain and less anxiety than did the control group.

It's an understandable response to try to make an unpleasant situation go away, but sometimes we have to be in unpleasant situations. And resisting them only amplifies the unpleasantness.

Acceptance makes us stronger. Most of us habitually try to avoid pain—emotional, physical, any kind. That's healthy in extreme circumstances. It keeps us alive. It keeps us away from danger. But many of us spend a disproportionate amount of our lives avoiding pain—shifting our posture when we feel the slightest discomfort, or engaging in coping mechanisms or distractions when we think or feel something uncomfortable. Every moment and ounce of energy we spend on avoidance, we drain from engaging in anything that could help us reach our goal. There's an opportunity cost to avoidance.

Let's take a very simple example. You're studying, and you feel slightly hungry, slightly bored, and slightly discouraged. It would be so easy to want to protect yourself from those feelings and go get something to eat, watch TV, anything to not feel those things. This process often happens below your level of consciousness. You may just find yourself walking to the kitchen or turning on the TV, without remembering getting up.

Or let's say that after spending a couple of minutes on an algebra problem for homework, you start to get frustrated because you don't think you can figure out the answer.

You know you should stay with it to try to discover the answer on your own for another minute or so. But you know that the answers in the back of the book are a few pages away, offering you some respite from the uncomfortable feeling of not knowing. At the same time, this respite will also rob you of a deeper learning experience—discovering the answer on your own. This is just one of many situations that would benefit from your acceptance.

If you're mindful of the unpleasantness, it's possible to just feel and notice and accept it. *Oh, this is boredom and hunger and discouragement. It feels unpleasant.* And that's it! Sometimes there's nothing else you have to do. Accept it as it is. Then continue your studying. Your driver gets to make the call about what to do. You can begin to treat unpleasant emotions and sensations as the bucket of ice water.

Happiness Is Around the Corner

As you practice mindfulness more, you will likely discover how many preferences your mind has: *I want this. I dislike this. I like that. I really want that.* The job of dislike is to find things to separate from, and to tell you that separation will bring happiness. The job of wanting is to find things to get, and to tell you having those things will bring happiness. Your job, the driver's job, is to get to know the job description of dislike and of wanting.

One of my students described her experience with the false promises of wanting: "I have so many projects, one after the other. And I get some relief after I finish one, but then I have another to do. I want to enjoy the journey, but I don't let myself until I complete a task, but then there's just another task."

As a kid, I used to play an arcade game called Whack-a-Mole, during which you swing this big fuzzy bat to bop little plastic moles that pop up out of a dozen or so holes in front of you. The moles tend to disappear as soon as they appear, so it's difficult to bop them in time. Living in the mode of having to accomplish endless tasks to be happy is like playing

Whack-a-Mole all the time. Every task that pops up is a task that needs to be completed. There is a feeling of relief when that task is completed, only to be interrupted by the knowledge of another task that needs to be completed, and so on.

Wanting

The experience of *wanting* is universal. It's natural and necessary. But in my experience, wanting generally has one of two connotations. One tends to cause suffering. The other doesn't. The first is some version of *This moment will be better when I get xyz*. We'll call this *must-having*. The latter is some version of *This moment is fine, and xyz would also be nice*. Let's call this version *aspiring*.

Must-having leads to stress and misery. It's a never-ending cycle. The more we get, the more we want. We get addicted to the high of accomplishment and attainment. So we want it again and again. Must-having induces a sense of lack. A sense of *this moment is not enough until xyz*. If we believe that happiness is always just around the corner, we operate in a must-having mode. Aspiring, however, acknowledges that this moment is enough just as it is and that there is always room for growth and improvement.

It can be hard to discern which type of wanting we are experiencing. I encourage you to observe the different flavors of must-having and aspiring in your own mind. In my experience, must-having can feel tense, pressured, and small. We may notice beliefs about not having enough or not being enough. Must-having usually invites in several passengers that agree with the notion that we are not enough, that this moment is not enough. The body approaches the edges of our window of tolerance when we really believe must-having thoughts. In contrast, aspiring feels uplifting, opening, and inspiring. Beliefs of hope and optimism and planning arise. Aspiring allows the journey itself to be enjoyable.

Most things we want have some version of both must-having and aspiring. But it's important to know which ones are at play. Which type of wanting do you experience when you think of test prep, or wanting to do well, or wanting to get into school? Take a moment to check. When you imagine those things, what does it feel like in your body?

While it's natural and okay if must-having is present, I recommend that you find and stay in touch with your aspiration, as it is typically a more sustainable and meaningful form of wanting.

Making Mental Grooves

Have you ever tried to saw a piece of wood with a hand saw? You first make a pencil or pen mark on the wood, marking where the saw should cut. You then place the base of the saw, the part of the toothed blade closest to your hand, on that mark. You then slowly pull the saw back toward you, causing each saw tooth to cut into that pencil mark. Each tooth makes the cut deeper, so you have to spend less and less effort guiding the saw. It sort of just stays in the groove by itself.

But what often happens is, while drawing the saw back, one of the saw teeth will sort of bounce the saw over a millimeter or two. Before you know it, there's a small cut in the wood a few millimeters over from the pencil mark. You have to pull the saw out of the new groove, and try to remake a groove on the pencil mark, but it is very difficult. The saw just wants to go into the already-made groove next to the pencil mark. So it keeps slipping into the wrong groove. It takes patience and persistence to form a groove next to one that already exists.

That's what it's like for our minds to form new habits or break old ones. This is good news and bad news. The bad news is that it's difficult to form new grooves. Our minds want to slide back into old ones, just as the saw wants to revert to the first groove made. The good news is that every single time we engage in a "good" habit, that habit becomes easier. Our mind more naturally engages in it. In neuroscience, this principle is called "what fires together wires together." Neural firings create pathways that "wire" together, making those pathways more default.

One of my well-worn paths is worrying about how to practice mindfulness correctly. But, as I explained above, worrying just trains my mind to worry. One way to break the worry pattern is to become mindful of the worry itself. Then I'm just practicing mindfulness.

A close cousin to worry is planning. In fact, sometimes we think we're planning, but we're actually worrying. When preparing for an interview, an athletic game, a confrontation, or a test, have you ever found yourself endlessly spinning about how you would perform? All you're doing is training your mind to plan.

This presents somewhat of a paradox, because without some planning, we wouldn't get anything done. So we need to balance the two: planning for the future and living in the moment. Most of us plan far more than we live in the present moment, so we need to strengthen our ability to live in the present. If either one is out of balance, we fall short of our goal. For example, a hiker needs to periodically look up at the summit for direction and inspiration. But if she doesn't allocate attention to walking, she will trip or wander astray. Conversely, if she never looks at the summit, she could walk in the opposite direction without knowing it.

So I invite you to periodically check in to see what kind of mental groove you are making. Ask yourself, *Do I aspire for my current mind state to become a mental groove?*

Framing

I was shooting basketball earlier today and remembered that as a kid, I ended every practice by making a shot. If I ended practice without making shot, it was bad luck. But there was no objective truth to my superstition. It was just a story I told myself. I made it my truth. Today, I thought about leaving the court after a missed shot rather than a made shot. What if I created a positive meaning around ending on a missed shot? So, as a thought experiment, I told myself that missing the last shot would just increase my desire to get back on the court and practice. It worked. I missed a shot, and walked away, looking forward to the following day when I could make a shot. The making or missing of the shots was meaningless. It was the story I told myself about those shots—the way I framed the experience—that held the power.

One important opportunity for framing arises when you check your answers to practice problems you've tried. Most people do something like this:

1. Do practice problem.
2. Check answer.
3a. If answer is correct, feel relief for about eight milliseconds, then do the next problem.

OR

3b. If answer is wrong, feel a little bad, then continue on a little more discouraged.

We can improve both of the above responses.

Let's start with when you get it right. Several students discount their performance when they do well. Their passenger DisCount shows up and says that they just got lucky. But you can and should celebrate a correct answer. Use that positivity as a springboard to tackle the next problem, or better yet, to look deeper into the problem you got right to see if there is an even better way to solve it.

Conversely, students often respond to a wrong answer by berating themselves for missing the problem and/or by declaring that the wrong answer is further evidence that they are fundamentally bad test takers. Of course, both messages come from passengers. The first is a line from ShWoody (*You should have gotten that right!*) and the second is from Told Ya So (*Told ya you were gonna miss it*). An alternative response is to celebrate the opportunity to improve. In fact, getting answers wrong is essential for improving.

With the above framing, it's possible to celebrate both wrong and right answers. There are myriad opportunities during test prep to reframe in this fashion, and I encourage you to search for such opportunities. But I'd like to share one more opportunity with you: your attitude toward the test writers and the test itself.

I hear several students, and even teachers, describing the test as an adversary, describing the test writers as conniving, and framing the test as some big maze of booby traps. But that's just a story, not objectively true. Is it a helpful story? Does it help you perform better?

Another way to frame the situation, one that's at least as true as the former framing, is that the test writers are people like you and me. Some of my friends are test writers. They are bright, talented, and compassionate people. It is definitely true that they write problems containing shortcuts and secrets that are easy to miss. But who's to say the writers didn't insert those shortcuts for our benefit, hoping that we would find them? Maybe the test writers are like video game designers, who put in secret levels and codes. It is far more helpful to view them as talented designers who want us to find the beauty in their design than as adversaries who are trying to trick us.

Framing experiences in a positive way is not idealistic or wishful thinking. It's humility. The truth is that we don't know what's going to end up being good or bad for us. Perhaps you have had a breakup or a failed interview that you thought was the worst thing that could have happened to you at the time. But it ended up being something you are very grateful for now.

I once heard a story about a man who used to row his boat to and from an island every day. One morning, about five minutes into his journey, the weather suddenly and drastically changed. It began storming. The wind was against him and caused the waves to rock the boat. The sideways rain blinded him. The normally one-hour journey took him four. He arrived to the island exhausted and discouraged. By the time he started the return journey that afternoon, the weather had cleared. The water was smooth, and the wind was still. He rowed back with ease.

Which was the "better" trip? Which one was more beneficial to him? You could make an argument either way. During the first trip, he strengthened his physical and mental stamina, but it was scary and unenjoyable. During the second, he reached his goal in time, felt peaceful, and connected with his surroundings, but he wasn't challenged.

What else can you frame in a more helpful way?

Equanimity

Meditators are often portrayed as being particularly equanimous. Equanimity is to take things in stride. It's an acceptance that we don't control everything, and that sometimes things we don't like will happen.

Over the past year, I've guided one of my students, Rachel, through the work of the previous chapters. She recently had an epiphany of sorts:

"I hate orange candy. But whether I like it or not, a few orange Sour Patch Kids are always going to be in the box. Similarly, negative thoughts are always gonna be in my mind. So are positive ones. It's absurd to let the occurrence of one or the other run your day. It's not about getting rid of negative thoughts or trying to have positive ones. It's about your relationship to those thoughts. If I follow my impulse to believe the thought or to fight the thought, I regret it. It's better to see that thought and not do anything about it. Without fuel, without energy, without resistance, that thought just hangs out and leaves on its own. But it takes training to do this."

Just as leg strength is a natural byproduct of playing many sports, equanimity is a natural byproduct of mindfulness practice. And just as there are specific exercises to increase leg strength, there are specific exercises to increase equanimity. Here's one of my favorites.

 **EXERCISE**

Equanimity

Whatever posture you're in is fine, as long as you're comfortable. Take a slow, deep breath. Then silently, or aloud, say the following:

There will be confusion, and clarity

There will be self-doubt, and confidence

There will be fatigue, and energy

And that's okay

Repeat the phrases above at your own pace. You can even allow your mind and body to somewhat adopt each adjective when you say it. When you say *clarity*, you can try to feel a little clarity. When you say *confidence*, you can try to feel confidence. Most importantly, when you say *that's okay*, try to feel what it's like to be okay.

You can time the phrases with the breaths for a more concentrated experience.

(breathe in) There will be confusion, (breathe out) and clarity

(breathe in) There will be self-doubt, (breathe out) and confidence

(breathe in) There will be fatigue, (breathe out) and energy

(breathe in) And that's okay (breathe out)

You can also drop many of the filler words.

(breathe in) confusion, (breathe out) clarity

(breathe in) self-doubt, (breathe out) confidence

(breathe in) fatigue, (breathe out) energy

(breathe in) that's okay (breathe out)

Feel free to choose your own words and phrases. The point is to choose two words that exist on two ends of a spectrum, such as hot and cold. Repeating to yourself that both ends of every spectrum are natural and will happen, helps you take those events in stride when they do occur.

Fatigue

Students frequently ask me what to do about mental fatigue. They say that their minds and bodies just start to shut down while studying or taking a test. Sometimes fatigue is due to lifestyle. No matter how much you psych yourself out, if your diet, sleep, and exercise schedule is insufficient, your mind will be tired.

Excessive stress and rumination throughout the day can also fatigue the mind. Every time we practice mindfulness, by noticing that we are lost in thought and returning to the present moment, we are saving ourselves from expending unnecessary mental energy. Many people on long mindfulness retreats start to need less and less sleep, sometimes down to just two or three hours a night. It's not just because the body is resting. The mind is also resting. You don't have to be on a mindfulness retreat to offer your mind moments of respite. Spending as little as one minute noticing the sensation of your breath or the sensations in your feet can give your mind a recharge.

Even if you are doing all you can to eat healthy, exercise, sleep well, and practice mindfulness, life still happens. Sometimes you have to study after a long day at school or work. Sometimes you don't have time to get eight or nine hours of sleep a night. So what should you do in the middle of studying or mindfulness when the mind fatigues?

The first thing is to really investigate whether it's actually boredom disguised as fatigue. Have you ever sat through a lecture, thinking you were going to pull your hair out or fall asleep only to get a jolt of energy when you were let out of class? That fatigue wasn't due to a lack of sleep. It was due to boredom.

I have found that the best in-the-moment cure for fatigue or boredom is curiosity. Curiosity gives rise to energy. That's why I urge you to bring curiosity to your mindfulness practice. The breath can be boring, but as soon as you watch it with curiosity, it's not boring. In fact, nothing is intrinsically boring. You may find a brick boring. But is a brick boring to a child who has never seen a brick? Our attitude toward an object or activity is more responsible for our interest level than is the object or the activity.

You can bring that same curiosity to your mindfulness practice, or even to elements of the test. There are innumerable things to be curious about while doing a practice problem. Am I going to get this right? What was the test writer trying to get me to think about here? How does my mind work when I'm challenged? What would happen if this problem were changed in a subtle way? What is the ideal way to do this problem?

Curiosity also gives rise to care. And when we care about something, our best selves tend to arise.

 **EXERCISE**

Being Curious

Take a deep breath. On a slow exhale, allow your shoulders to fall away from your ears.

Imagine that you are an alien consciousness that just woke up in the body that you have now. That you have never ever felt the sensations in the body that your consciousness now occupies.

Imagine that your task is to be able to report what it feels like to be in the human body that you're now in. Allow your awareness to explore different areas of your body as a child would explore different areas of a new playground. What "color" are things? How hard or soft are things? Which places seem inviting? Which don't?

Spend the next few minutes exploring. It's best to close your eyes.

I'm going to do this exercise now and document my experience below for reference. However, I'd encourage you to do it yourself before reading my account.

Awareness goes to right side of the neck, which is hot, sharp, burning. Right shoulder just relaxed and dropped on its own. Brought awareness to the eyes, which also relaxed on their own. That's kind of interesting. Now told the awareness to go to the toes. I feel them, but don't know how to describe them. Tingly I guess. Now I feel the whole chest. Tightness in throat. Now letting my awareness go where it wants. Head, now toes, now skin all over body. Now it's trying to go outside of my body, but I can't really feel anything there. Get a sense of spaciousness when it tries to go there, though. Seems like a lot of space in my body now. Hollow. Everything feels alive in most parts.

Take a moment to note something that you noticed about your body or awareness that you had never noticed before.

I once heard someone ask Joseph, "What has kept you practicing for fifty years?" Joseph said, "Curiosity. I'm still so curious about how the mind works. What could be more fascinating?"

See what happens if you bring a little curiosity to your daily activities—to brushing your teeth, to conversations, to mindfulness practice, to the studying process. I think you'll be amazed at the energy and concentration that can follow.

Standing and walking mindfulness practices are great ways to alleviate fatigue, because they energize your body and give you new objects to be curious about.

 **EXERCISE**

Standing and Walking Practice

Go ahead and stand up. Keep this book in one hand and rest the other on something for balance.

Notice the pressure of your feet on the floor. Notice pressure on various parts of your feet—the ball of your left foot . . . left heel . . . ball of right foot . . . right heel.

Notice how, if you try to stand still, dozens of tiny muscles in your feet and ankles fire on their own to keep you balanced.

You can slightly rock back and forth to see how the sensations change. You can also shift your weight from one foot to the other.

If your mind wanders, bring it back to the sensations in your feet.

As you shift your weight back and forth, you can begin to slowly, very slowly, walk in place. Notice how the sensations in your feet change with each micromovement.

You can experiment with walking back and forth. Take five or ten paces, noticing every movement of your feet. Pause. Feel the sensations of turning around. Then walk back to your starting place. And repeat.

You can implement standing and walking mindfulness practices throughout your day. Simply pay attention to the sensations of your feet when you're standing in line or walking from point A to point B.

Anything can be made into a mindfulness practice. I invite you to explore what other hobbies and/or activities you can make into mindfulness practices.

Proud Sponge

During one class at Harvard, a professor showed us a five-minute video of a single kernel of popcorn popping, with the camera zoomed in on one kernel and the film speed at about 1/30 of normal. But she didn't tell us that we were looking at a popcorn kernel.

My fellow students and I engaged in an implicitly understood race to figure out what in the world the yellow shimmery blob on the screen was. My mind raced to form hypotheses about what it was then used the subsequent moments of the video to either confirm or deny those hypotheses. I thought it was a lemon at one point, then someone's skin, then a planet. But each time I came to a conclusion, further data made me correct my assumption.

The interesting thing to me was just how obsessed I was with figuring out what the thing was on the screen. I had to know. Even if it meant forming ill-informed hypotheses, with no consequence to waiting to figure it out. My body was tense with anticipation. About four minutes in, I realized that the figure on the screen was popcorn. I experienced about two seconds of happiness and relief, then I was bored. Four minutes of unpleasantness for two seconds of joy. Upon reflection, I realized that it wasn't the desire to know what was on screen that had gripped me so much, but the discomfort of not knowing.

But that tension and discomfort didn't help me figure anything out. I had added unnecessary stress to the situation. Granted, four minutes of tension wasn't very taxing on my mind and body, but many of you are in a four-*month* process.

It is possible to both relax and fervently pursue a goal. But it also takes a firm belief that it's okay to not know along the way. The truth is that you often won't know things, so you may as well be okay with it.

When I was on the three-month mindfulness retreat, I approached Joseph with several problems that were rooted in not knowing. He had taught me all kinds of techniques, as the other teachers did. But as you may have noticed in this book, there are infinite ways and combinations with which to carry out those techniques. So I would get paralyzed when I didn't know exactly how to be with an emotion or thought that was arising. *How long should I pay attention to it? Should I feel it more in my body or in my mind? What if there are two things arising at once? How do I deal with all of these questions right now?* Joseph said, "I have a new phrase for you: *It's okay to not know.*" I paused, looked down, looked back up, and said, "But no it's not!"

I still have trouble with not knowing. It's understandable, because most of us grew up getting tested on what we do know. But just because we're in the pursuit of knowledge doesn't mean we have to be ashamed about the pursuit itself, which is predicated on curiosity, which is predicated on not knowing. At our Harvard Graduate School of Education orientation, one professor said one of the smartest things you can do is to embrace not knowing. "Nodding along with a teacher or fellow classmates, pretending you know, is just doing yourself a disservice. Relinquish the idea that you do or should know more than you do right now. That's just a barrier to future learning."

One of my students, Anna, had a resistance to reviewing her homework problems. She often understood problems well enough to get them right, but not well enough to feel comfortable with them. Unsurprisingly, her progress stagnated. I said, "Anna, you understand 75 percent of this problem. Why don't you review it until you understand it 100 percent?" She replied, "Because doing that part is uncomfortable. I don't like not knowing. So I learn enough to get it right, then move on." I can relate to Anna. Why would we get a problem right only to tell ourselves we still don't know enough about it? We don't want to sink into that murky feeling of not knowing.

As soon as you wholeheartedly admit that you don't know, it opens up tremendous space for learning. Make it a practice to celebrate not knowing. Seek out things that you don't know. Say to your friends, teachers, peers, "Tell me more about that." The smartest people I know ask the most questions. And remember, when you ask questions, chances are somebody else has those same questions but is too afraid to ask. As Albert Einstein said, "The important thing is not to stop questioning." Be a proud sponge.

CHAPTER 4

Driver's Ed

Why Do We Need Driver's Ed?

Mindfulness practice allows us to see the cause and effect of things more clearly. We begin to see the habits of our mind that cause suffering. Over time, we begin to naturally choose not to pursue, or repeat, those habits, encouraging a more clear and positive state of mind. But there are ways to more overtly and actively encourage positive mind states.

When I first told students that I was going to write about "soft stuff," such as kindness and gratitude, they resisted: "I don't care if I feel good during the test prep process. I just want to do well on the test!" They have a point. Most of you reading this book have a clear and narrowly defined goal—to perform well on a standardized test. We must ask ourselves, do positive mind states increase performance?

Imagine that you are going to study for two hours, and that you get to choose between the following two scenarios:

Scenario 1: You feel good, optimistic, happy, and grateful. You feel alert and relaxed.

Scenario 2: You feel anxious and angry. You feel discouraged and ashamed.

Given the opportunity, which scenario would you choose? If you chose Scenario 1, as most students do, take a moment to think about why. Would you choose it only because it would be a more pleasant experience for you? Do you also think it would lead to more productivity and learning? Why?

If learning and productivity were even a slight factor in your decision, and your goal is to achieve a higher score, it stands to reason that it is incumbent upon you to cultivate positive mind states. While there is an argument to be made for well-being as the end goal, that's not what this book is about. I'm making the case for well-being in service of performance. The common ancillary benefits—improved social relationships, enhanced well-being, better sleep, etc.—are just icing on the cake.

One way to view our internal experience is in terms of positive and negative mind states. The driver leads to positive mind states, and passengers, when not seen or when believed, lead to negative mind states. We have discussed how to identify and work with passengers to reduce their negative impact, but focusing solely on passengers is not enough. We have to train the driver as well.

Consider this analogy: One way to eliminate weeds in a yard is to plant grass seed. Another way is to pull weeds. If you only plant grass seed, you may still have a lot of weeds. If you only pull weeds, you may be left with a yard of only dirt. The best approach is to both plant grass seed and pull weeds. Think of driver's ed as planting grass seed, and think of working with passengers (*not* getting rid of passengers) as pulling weeds.

The grass itself acts as a buffer. The more grass there is, the less room there is for weeds to grow. Similarly, the stronger the driver is, the less often passengers will take the wheel. Even if you are an expert at working with your passengers, without a strong driver, passengers will just take turns grabbing the wheel.

Of the numerous positive mind states and numerous ways to cultivate those mind states, I will only focus on one—kindness toward oneself, or *self-kindness*. Self-kindness is not only underdeveloped in most of us, but it is also a prerequisite for many other positive mind states. If we don't feel supported and safe to some degree, our mental energy and faculties are allocated to self-protection, which can preclude us from feeling kindness toward others. Most of us rely on others for support and safety, but what happens when other people are in a bad mood or are unavailable? We need to provide ourselves with support and safety, and a potent way to do that is through self-kindness. You are capable of doing this, proven by your ability to help another person in difficult times—something you have likely done at least once in your life.

Another reason self-kindness deserves special attention is that it is uniquely unchecked. There are inherent checks and balances with other, outward-facing, positive mind states, such as kindness toward others. If we aren't kind toward others, there are immediate social consequences. But there are no official or unofficial restrictions on how cruel we can be toward ourselves. No one else hears the belittling whispers of our minds, so no one else can step in. We can endlessly berate ourselves without consequence.

Ideally, kindness should be object-blind—a pervasive quality that shines in all directions, landing on anything in its path, whether human, animal, or even inanimate objects. So my hope for you, and for me, is that one day we can drop the "self" prefix to kindness. But right now, we need it to highlight the most deserted recipient of kindness—yourself.

Recently, I taught a few five-week mindfulness workshops to test prep students. Most students reported that the week on self-kindness was the most impactful of all. It surprised me to learn that most students actually already knew how hard they were on themselves, yet still chose to engage in self-criticism. If you are ever purposefully self-critical, reflect on your own reasons for why. Whatever the reason, the most important question is, Does it work? What I mean by *work* is, Does it bring out the best in you?

When I asked my students why they continued the self-criticism, the answer was unanimously some version of "If I don't berate myself, I will become complacent and won't improve."

We all know that this approach rarely works with other people, yet we continue to engage in it with ourselves. My students will protest, "But what about tough love!?" It's an important question. You may be recalling times when a coach or a parent was hard on you, effectively inspiring you to achieve. The difference is that those examples of tough love made you feel inspired or motivated in some way. If that's the case, there's nothing wrong with tough love. How you talk to yourself should be a means to an end. That end should be embodying your full potential, not only as a performer, but as a person. So whenever you're trying to justify the harsh criticism you submit yourself to, ask yourself, *Does it make me feel inspired?* If so, by all means, proceed. But people often justify their self-criticism as being tough love, even when they don't feel the love part. If you choose the tough love route, great, but remember that tough love has two words.

Perhaps you have different people in your life who require different forms of motivation and inspiration. Some need encouragement. Some need a logical approach. Some need an emotional approach. Some just want you to listen. You have to know your audience to know what they need. Caring for yourself is no different. You have to know what you need. Most of us are less practiced at assessing our own needs than assessing those of others. You'll need to discover the brand of self-kindness that you need through trial and error. I encourage you to analyze how you physically feel, rather than what you think, during different self-kindness approaches. You will need to call upon your mindfulness techniques to do so. When we feel encouraged, we feel uplifted, open, tall, and/or energized. When we feel discouraged, we feel closed, sinking, small, and/or lethargic.

EXERCISE

Pep Talk

Imagine you're taking a walk in a park, and you notice a bunch of six-year-olds playing soccer. You decide to sit on a bench and watch for a bit. You see one of the boys dribble the ball through the defense, making his way toward the goal. He winds up to kick and completely misses the ball. His misguided kick has so much inertia that it sweeps him off his feet, causing him to fall. He's so embarrassed that he runs off the field and sits down in front of you with his head in his arms. You can hear him sobbing. What would you say to him?

Imagine saying this to the child, and imagine his reaction:

Everyone is looking at you and judging you. How could you be so clumsy? That was an easy ball to kick. Your friends wouldn't have messed up that badly. You're just not good at sports, so it's probably best not to try. Now you're just feeling sorry for yourself. Toughen up.

How did that feel to say in your mind? Do you think it would have been effective? Why or why not?

Before reading on, imagine saying what you would actually say to that child.

Now ask yourself, if you were that child, what kind of pep talk would have worked better for you? How about now as an adult? Why should you missing a problem on a test be treated any differently than a child missing a kick?

Bring to mind something you've done in the past few days that sparked self-criticism. Now write a short pep talk for yourself about that situation.

Even if we know what kind of pep talk we need from ourselves, paradoxically, it's often hardest to access our self-kindness when we need it the most. Additionally, many people actively resist self-kindness, because they conflate engaging in self-kindness with indulging in it. I have never met anyone, ever, who has overindulged in self-kindness. Most of us experience such a deficit that we forget we're even deserving of it. As Galway Kinnell writes in his poem "Saint Francis and the Sow": "Sometimes it's necessary to reteach a thing its loveliness."

Six Components of Driver's Ed

Whenever you're stuck, I recommend addressing one or more of the following aspects of self-kindness. You can treat these aspects like colors when painting. Use your artistic license to use any or all of the below, in any combination, to paint whatever self-kindness picture you'd like.

1. It's not your fault
2. You're not alone
3. Care and well-wishing
4. Gratitude
5. Receiving goodness
6. Humor

1. It's Not Your Fault

Have you ever been walking somewhere, then found yourself jumping back in fear from something you saw on the path in front of you? Maybe you saw a snake, or a stick that looks like a snake? Have you noticed that, in those situations, your body often responds before "you" have time to consciously process the situation? Our bodies continually operate without our conscious direction. Our stomachs digest food. Our eyes blink. Our mouths salivate. And our minds produce thoughts and emotions.

Some biologists believe that all thoughts and emotions occur a split second before conscious awareness notices them. Do you agree with that? See for yourself. For the next thirty seconds, try not to have any thoughts or emotions, but notice which ones arise on their own. Try this before reading on.

Regarding the thoughts that popped up, did you ask for them to arise? And even if you did, did you ask for the asking to arise?

Thoughts and emotions often, if not always, occur on their own volition. They don't ask our permission. As soon as we really know this, through repeated observation, thoughts such as *I shouldn't feel this way* and *I shouldn't think this* become apparently nonsensical. Don't confuse blame and fault for responsibility. It is possible to be responsible without being at fault. For example, a thought popped into my head, just now, of a unicorn on roller skates. Can I fairly be blamed for that? Thoughts and emotions are kind of like unordered packages that arrive on your doorstep. They aren't your fault, but they are your responsibility.

There's a powerful scene in the movie *Good Will Hunting* involving Will, played by Matt Damon, and his therapist Sean, played by Robin Williams. Will had been through a lot as a child, and at the end of one of their sessions, Sean said to Will, "It's not your fault." Will shrugged it off and said, "I know." Sean repeated himself. "It's not your fault." Again, Will said, "I know." Sean, sensing that Will wasn't really hearing him, repeated himself with more intensity, "It's not your fault." Will became agitated, again saying that he knew. As Sean kept repeating it, Will heard those words on deeper and deeper levels, eventually breaking down crying in Sean's arms.

During stressful journeys such as test prep we sometimes have to be as persistent with ourselves as Sean was with Will. That, in turn, frees up tremendous mental space to address the only relevant question to ask when we experience hardship: *How can I work with what's happening right now?*

I use the phrase *of course* to help remind me that my mental and emotional arisings aren't my fault. I first heard it from meditation teacher Andrea Fella, who said that the phrase helps her view everything that happens as a natural consequence of infinite previous causes and conditions. "*Of course* that passenger arose when I missed a problem, because xyz." Even if you can't identify the xyz, there is an xyz. There are always reasons. *Of course* is not a surrender to a deterministic view of the future, but it is an acknowledgment that whatever arose in the past or what is arising right now is the natural result of infinite causes and conditions that we can't always trace and identify.

Another phrase that serves a similar purpose is *and that's okay*. Meeting whatever we notice with *and that's okay* helps to preempt and prevent the natural negative and critical bias we can have against ourselves when doing a seemingly neutral exercise, such as naming whatever we noticed during a basic meditation practice. Sometimes we may name a passenger but have a subtle belief that the passenger's very arising is not okay. Saying *and that's okay* explicitly trains our minds not to fight against the present moment and not to fight against ourselves. Accepting whatever arises in our experience is a radical act of self-kindness.

EXERCISE

And That's Okay

This can be done in any posture, doing any activity. Take a deep breath, allowing the muscles in your body to relax. Rather than choosing an anchor for your attention to rest on, allow your attention to land on whatever it wants.

One way to prompt this orientation of mindfulness practice is to ask yourself, *Am I aware? Aware of what?*

Whatever your awareness notices, internally say to yourself *and that's okay*.

For example, if you notice a sound, rather than labeling it *sound,* say to yourself *and that's okay*. If you notice a thought telling you that you're not doing this exercise correctly, say to yourself *and that's okay*. But it's important that you don't address the content of the thought, but *the having* of the thought. If you find yourself wondering, getting impatient, getting frustrated, or anything, notice it and say *and that's okay*. Even if you have the thought *this is not okay*, notice that thought and say *and that's okay*.

Reflect on what situations during your test prep process you think you could use this technique the most.

2. You're Not Alone

As we realize how our own thoughts and emotions work, we begin to empathize and connect with others more, realizing we are not all that different. We can start to question how we blame others. We can start to wonder what the difference is between blaming someone and holding them responsible. Zen master Thich Nhat Hanh beautifully highlights a common misconception of fault and blame in this excerpt from his poem, "Call Me by My True Names":

> *I am the frog swimming happily in the clear pond,*
>
> *and I am also the grass-snake who, approaching in silence, feeds itself on the frog.*
>
> *Please call me by my true names.*

I once heard someone say, "If you traded places with someone else, atom for atom, and had experienced their history, would you not have made the same choices as them?"

When we have empathy and compassion for others, we feel more connected to them. When we feel more connected, we feel less alone and less guarded. When we feel less guarded, we are more able to be our full selves, reaching our full potential, performance related or otherwise.

Any negative experience can be amplified by a feeling of aloneness. If we miss a problem, it doesn't feel good, but if we are the only person in the class who misses a problem, it really doesn't feel good. Many of us assume aloneness when we experience negative emotions, simply because we don't see evidence that others are experiencing anything but happiness. Most of us put on happy faces around other people, especially on social media. It's no wonder we feel alone, when every picture posted by our friends makes them look like the happiest people on earth.

But we all experience negative setbacks and emotions. We need to actively remember that we aren't alone. We are all in this together but tend to think we're fighting life's battles alone. We're not. As Albert Einstein wrote, "A human being . . . experiences himself, his thoughts and feelings as something separated from the rest—a kind of optical delusion of his consciousness." When I find myself feeling alone, I can take some solace in knowing that I'm buying into a delusion.

It can be helpful to reflect on the plight of others, but only in a way that sees their suffering as part of ours, and in a way that seeks to feel compassion for others and ourselves. Have you ever heard someone say, "Who cares if you xyz? At least you aren't starving!" Some of you may use this logic on yourselves at times, trying to shame your way into gratitude. You have to be very careful when you reflect on others' suffering. If it makes you feel alone and ashamed rather than connected and compassionate, alter your approach or try again later.

EXERCISE

You Are Not Alone

Take a moment to identify an unpleasant emotion or thought that you are experiencing. Don't go into a thought story about it, but do feel it in the body.

Reflect on the fact that millions and millions of people throughout history have felt the exact same brand of suffering that you are experiencing now.

Reflect on the fact that there are likely many people in the world at this very moment who share your particular brand of suffering.

Reflect on the fact that one or more of the people you care most about have felt something similar to what you feel now.

What other reflection helps you feel less alone?

3. Care And Well-Wishing

I am combining care and well-wishing, because I think they go hand in hand. If you care about someone, you wish them well. If you wish someone well, you care about them.

How can you tell when someone cares about you? Is it the words they say? How it feels to be around them? How do you know when you care for someone else?

If you don't feel cared for, or if you don't feel like someone has your back, you can feel alone and defensive, sapping your performance potential. I will give you a few techniques to express care toward yourselves, but I encourage you to develop and practice whatever form of self-care techniques work for you.

Touch stimulates the release of oxytocin, often referred to as the love hormone. Oxytocin causes feelings of interpersonal warmth and connectedness. Most of us rely on touch from others, but it's also possible for us to stimulate oxytocin release from self-touch, experiencing *intra*personal connectedness and warmth. One way is to literally give yourself a hug. Go ahead and try it right now. If you're around people, it will just look like you're stretching your shoulders or like you're cold. Wrap your arms around yourself for about twenty seconds.

I find the best way to express self-care is by combining touch, imagery, words, and sentiment.

 **EXERCISE**

Self-care and Well-wishing

Bring to mind a plant, animal, or person that you can't help but caringly smile when thinking of. For the purposes of this exercise, it's probably best not to choose a person with whom you have a particularly complicated relationship.

While holding the image of this being in your mind, allow yourself to smile and feel the sensations of care in your body. Spend a few minutes holding both the image of that person and the sensations of care toward them in your mind. Now repeat the following phrases, either silently or aloud:

May you be safe

May you be happy

May you be healthy

May you live with ease

You can time these phrases with the breath—the first part of each phrase on the in-breath, the second part of each phrase on the out-breath. If you choose to say or think the phrases, your attention should be loosely holding three things: the feelings you are experiencing, the image of the being, and the words themselves.

Now replace the image of that person with an image of yourself. This image can be of yourself now or of you as a child. Picturing yourself as a child can allow self-kindness to flow more easily. Repeat the following phrases:

May I be safe

May I be happy

May I be healthy

May I live with ease

It's normal and okay for this exercise to catalyze the presence of a few passengers. If that happens, just notice the passengers and return to the image of yourself and feelings of kindness toward yourself.

If you would like, you can now widen the scope of well-wishing to include all beings.

May we be safe

May we be happy

May we be healthy

May we live with ease

4. Gratitude

Gratitude is one of the most extensively researched qualities that leads to happiness. Gratitude practice has been shown to improve relationships, improve self-esteem, increase happiness, decrease envy, decrease depression, and decrease anxiety. I have found gratitude practice to be the most efficient antidote to negative mind states.

Though we may not always feel grateful, the embers of gratitude are ever-present within each of us. As my philosophy teacher Houman Harouni once told me, "Find the embers. Blow on them. Nurture them. Make no mistake, they are there. You would not be alive if they weren't."

 **EXERCISE**

Embers of Gratitude

Search your body and mind for any embers of gratitude— big or small. It's okay if you don't find anything immediately. Patiently search. Gratitude can be disguised by a neutral feeling, caused by years of taking something for granted. For example, most of us feel neutral towards the breath. But it only takes a few seconds without it to highlight our gratitude for it.

Once you find something you're grateful for, hold that image in your mind and connect with any feeling of gratitude you have. Get to know that feeling. Give it space to permeate your body and mind.

As fuel for the feeling, you can lightly hold the mental image of the object of your gratitude and mentally say the phrase, *I'm grateful for* _____. Repeat the phrase as often as needed to serve the feeling of gratitude.

Once you have spent a couple of minutes on one object of gratitude, find another.

Continue for five to ten minutes.

Gratitude practice habituates the mind to look for positive experiences. A mind that more frequently looks for positive experiences, more frequently finds positive experiences.

5. Receiving Goodness

Earlier, I mentioned meditation teacher Brian Lasage. A few years ago, he told me story about a car ride he took with his co-teacher after leading a weekend retreat. His co-teacher, who also happened to be Brian's mentor, looked at Brian and said, "We did a good thing." Brian kind of shrugged off the compliment, saying, "Yeah, I guess so." When telling me this story, Brian shared the surprise at the seriousness with which his mentor retorted, "Brian, we did a good thing. It's important that you let that in."

That story has stuck with me for years, because I realized how often I act like Brian. My DisCount passenger dismisses the good things that I do, and I believe that passenger. But celebrating the good is important, because it encourages more good. And more importantly, it's true. It can be scary to pat ourselves on the back, or prop ourselves up, because we can think that someone might quickly tear us down. But that fear is separate from the fact that you did a good thing.

Rick Hanson, the psychologist I mentioned earlier, has written and spoken extensively about the importance of "taking in the good." Rick reminds us that it usually takes several good interactions to balance out one bad one, that we usually work harder to not lose $100 than to earn $100 that we don't have, that we generally remember negative experiences more than positive ones, and that our minds are like Velcro for negative experiences and Teflon for positive ones. Do you find that to be the case in your experience?

If this is the case for you, you need to make a conscious effort to notice and absorb the good. In doing so, you may feel like you are being unbalanced or somehow being unfair to the negative experiences. You may fear that you are being blind to the negative experiences. But I have never seen that to be the case. I think you can rest assured that you're in no danger of recognizing and feeling too much good.

I had such a difficult time admitting and letting in my own goodness that I started keeping a list of genuine compliments people give me. When people express gratitude toward me, I write it down. Otherwise, I would discount and forget about it. That's not only unfair to myself, but it's unfair to the other person who expressed authentic thoughts toward me. Why should I value that person's negative thoughts more than the positive ones? When my passengers are running rampant, consulting the list can wake up the driver.

I recommend engaging in these three methods of receiving goodness:

- Actively think about a scenario in which you have done good, and feel the bodily effects.
- When good things happen, especially when you do something good, make a conscious effort to savor and feel them.
- When you do something good, or receive a compliment, write it down. Consult that list at least once per week.

 **EXERCISE**

Receiving Goodness from Others

Imagine yourself in a place where you feel safe, happy, and comfortable. Imagine the details—the temperature, what you're wearing, what you see, etc.

Now imagine that two or three trusted beings join you in that place. These beings can be plants, animals, or people, alive or not. Imagine that they sit or stand across from you.

Imagine each one offering you care and support, in whatever way they know how. Focus on accepting their words or energy. Allow your reaction to be as it is. Sometimes resistance can come up if we don't agree with the content of what we imagine them saying. Remember that you don't have to believe what they say. You just have to believe that they believe it.

Here are some phrases you can imagine them offering you:

I believe in you

I really see you, and I accept everything that I see

I know that you have a good heart and a capable mind

I know that you have always done the best you could with what you had at the time

If you'd like, you can imagine yourself joining them, looking back at yourself. Now you can offer yourself phrases of support.

EXERCISE

Receiving Goodness from Yourself

Find a comfortable position, either sitting or lying down. Take a few calming breaths, allowing your body to relax. Bring to mind something good you've done. It could be something as simple as holding the door open for someone or helping someone pick something up. It could be when you consoled someone. It could be something you did for yourself, such as going to the gym.

Imagine what it felt like during that act of goodness. Allow any discounting or rationalizing to just be there. See if you can tap into appreciation, joy, or connectedness you felt during that act of good. Let that feeling permeate your body and mind. Use the image and/or good feeling as your anchor for a few minutes.

Now consult your written list of appreciations about yourself. Read a few, bringing to mind the situations in which they occurred. Practice letting in the words on the page. Again, allow any potential passengers to come and go.

6. Humor

One day, about two months into the three-month retreat I attended at Insight Meditation Society, I saw an older woman struggling a little bit to push a wheelbarrow full of leaves and wood. I had the immediate impulse to help. Then I remembered that I was on a silent retreat. I wondered if helping her was more important than maintaining the silence. *Should I help her? Why do I want to help her? How am I supposed to be meditating with all of this mental activity right now? I'm about to pass her. What should I do? Here I go again, making a big deal out of nothing. I'm hopeless.*

All it took was seeing a woman with a wheelbarrow for me to conclude, in less than a minute, that I was hopeless. I relayed this story to Joseph during one of our semi-weekly fifteen-minute check-ins. I told him that I still didn't know what I should have done—that I was going back and forth about whether I should've helped her. Joseph casually interrupted my worried monologue, with a half-smile, "Eh, she was probably stronger than you anyway."

It was a risky move on his part, because I was pretty vulnerable, and I could feel part of me wanting to take offense. But I couldn't help but laugh. It was absurdly hilarious for that to be his "wise" response. But in hindsight, it was probably the wisest response possible.

What he had done without saying so was highlight just how seriously I was taking the situation, and myself. At the time, I thought it was a dilemma of epic proportions and immeasurable consequence. By giving a lighthearted answer, Joseph helped redirect my energy toward something more useful.

I understand that test prep is more consequential than my wheel barrow dilemma. But remember what my student Alessandro said: "There's a difference between something being important and something being serious." Humor is an essential component of self-kindness, as it often catalyzes a paradigm shift from a self-criticism spiral to a broader perspective. Next time you feel stressed during the test prep process (or otherwise), give yourself permission to playfully tease yourself, as you might a good friend. We all have these minds that do whatever they want without our permission. They will talk nonsense, play weird movies, make big deals out of little things, give us great advice, give us terrible advice, etc. If we took everything the mind does seriously, we'd go crazy! Sometimes we just have to greet it with a smile.

CHAPTER 5

Putting It All Together

Start Wherever You Are

I hope I have given you a solid foundation on which to build your own tailored approach to the other half of test prep.

The most important thing for you to do is start. Whether you are six months or six days away from the test, start now. Spend at least fifteen minutes per day working on something from this book, some aspect of the other half of test prep. When deciding exactly which techniques to use and when, rather than trying to figure out what you "should" do, choose what sparks the most interest and energy for you.

TAILS

You will also likely want to draw on some of the techniques in this book for acute, unpredictable, or intense situations. It can be difficult to think very clearly at such times, so it's helpful to have a go-to strategy, somewhat of a first-aid kit. Over the years, I have developed such a kit that I call TAILS, which stands for *Take a moment—Anchor—Inquire—Listen—Self-kindness.* Please feel free to use and/or edit TAILS to suit your own learning.

Take a Moment

When stressed, the last thing we want to do is pause. It feels like giving up, like not making progress. It allows the discomfort in our bodies and minds to take full hold of us. We think if we stop running, our shadow will catch up to us. But pausing breaks the cycle, it breaks whatever chain of passengers that is derailing us. If we sense that we are being led in the wrong direction and we're not sure which direction is correct, the best thing we can do is put the car in neutral for a moment—to stop accelerating. Pausing takes our foot off the gas.

Anchor

When stressed, several passengers are usually present. We are outside, or approaching the outside, of our window of tolerance. The momentum is going in a direction we don't want. Feeling or sensing something happening in the present moment can serve as an anchor, helping to prevent that momentum from picking back up without our knowledge. It's best not to anchor in an unpleasant feeling or thought, though.

Inquire

When stressed, there is often a message we aren't hearing. We need to ask which passenger is the loudest and what that passenger wants to say.

It's important to realize that asking the question itself is half of the answer, regardless of what answer comes. When stressed, we can feel like we are the passengers. But as soon as we ask a passenger a question, we are implicitly admitting to ourselves that we are not the passenger. If we were, how else could we be asking it a question?

Listen

When stressed, we don't want to hear anything potentially stressful. So this part takes courage. The messages of the passengers are not always pleasant to hear. Sometimes they are excruciating. But remember, the messages themselves are just symptoms of an underlying care for us. We have to be willing to hear the message and look for the care underneath. Otherwise, passengers don't feel heard. When they don't feel heard, they speak louder.

Self-kindness

When stressed, we need to rebuild the safety, security, trust, and optimism that passengers can tend to erode. Remember that these are core parts of us. They don't come and go. They only get covered up. To resurface them, you can do one of the Driver's Ed exercises, perhaps "Pep Talk" or "And That's Okay."

Signposts

As you go forward, I encourage you to continue to develop and listen to your driver, who has more wisdom *about you* than I, or anyone else, could. I spent years thinking that the answer to how I should work with *my* mind lies in someone *else's* mind. While it is true that I did need others to give me basic knowledge, as I have given you, I eventually learned that anything outside me could only serve as a signpost pointing me toward some truth within.

The words in this book are just signposts. Where and when they don't resonate, please feel free to disregard or come back to them later. My goal is for this book to prop you up, for you to be able to stand on it. Not for it to be another text that tells you what is right and wrong.

There is a path for you that leads to your full potential. I hope what I've shared in this book helps to light that path, one that I'm confident you would have found on your own anyway.